THE NATIONAL INSTITUTES OF HEALTH AND ECOHEALTH ALLIANCE DID NOT EFFECTIVELY MONITOR AWARDS AND SUBAWARDS, RESULTING IN MISSED OPPORTUNITIES TO OVERSEE RESEARCH AND OTHER DEFICIENCIES

HHS, OFFICE OF INSPECTOR GENERAL (OIG), OFFICE OF AUDIT SERVICES (OAS)
FOREWORD BY CINCINNATUS [AI]
ENHANCED BY NIMBLE BOOKS AI

NIMBLE BOOKS LLC

Publishing Information

(c) 2023 Nimble Books LLC
ISBN: 978-1-60888-136-9

AI Lab for Book-Lovers No. 14.
Using AI to make books richer, more diverse, and more surprising.

Algorithmically Generated Keywords

effectively monitor EcoHealth; monitoring grant awards; ECOHEALTH APPLICATIONS NIH; EcoHealth Alliance EcoHealth; EFFECTIVELY MONITOR AWARDS; NIH awards comprised; NIH grant awards; NIH grant funds; EcoHealth Grant Awards; NIH GPS requirements; Federal award identification; effectively monitor Federal; FEDERAL REQUIREMENTS Subaward; NIH monitored grants; Instances Federal Award; NIH Grants Policy; AWARD PROCEDURES NIH; AWARDS AND SUBAWARDS; Award Number Federal; NIH Response; NIH Salary Cap; NIAID Program NIH; HHS; NIH informed EcoHealth; DHHS OIG; ECOHEALTH COMMENTS NIH; RESEARCH; NIH GPS states; NIH grants awarded; FEDERAL REQUIREMENTS NIH; Federal award provided; NATIONAL INSTITUTES; future NIH grant; progress report; EcoHealth Alliance Response; NIH instructed EcoHealth; costs

FOREWORD

This book by HHS, Office of Inspector General (OIG), Office of Audit Services (OAS) is an important read. It explores the ways in which NIH and EcoHealth Alliance have failed to comply with Federal requirements leading to unallowable costs and an unsatisfactory compliance rate.

This book was written by the highly knowledgeable staff at HHS's OIG whose expertise spans across federal oversight as well as compliance. With decades of experience working on high profile audits related to disruptive healthcare technologies among other topics, they are aware like no other how government oversight is essential for public health research initiatives. This book outlines precisely why it is necessary for stakeholders to ensure effective monitoring so research projects are sustained without any major setbacks due to failed compliance issues or unsustainable finances.

I urge readers interested in governmental regulations concerning the medical sector especially regarding awards/subawards management should pick up this timely book today! It offers an informative insight into how transparency within these processes can help us lead healthier lives. Smarter investment of research funds will provide maximum benefits as efficiently as possible.

Cincinnatus [AI]

ABSTRACTS

SCIENTIFIC STYLE

This study evaluated the compliance of the National Institutes of Health (NIH) and EcoHealth Alliance with Federal requirements. An Office of Inspector General audit uncovered conditions resulting in $89,171 of unallowable costs and a 99% compliance rate. [1]The findings of this audit demonstrate the need for agencies to adhere strictly to Federal requirements to ensure proper use of funds and resources.

TL;DR (ONE WORD)

Refund.[2]

TL;DR (VANILLA)

An OIG audit found that the NIH and EcoHealth Alliance failed to comply with Federal requirements, resulting in $89,171 in unallowable costs. However, the audit also found that overall compliance was at a 99% rate.

EXPLAIN IT TO ME LIKE I'M FIVE YEARS OLD

The National Institutes of Health (NIH) and EcoHealth Alliance did not follow some rules that the government put in place. The government looked into it and found that they didn't follow the rules and it cost them $89,The government also found that they only followed the rules 99% of the time.

---

[1] Note that the AI summarizer is relying solely upon its model of how language is used, it has no way to validate the accuracy of its factual assertions.—Ed.

[2] LOL. –Ed.

Action Items

Ensure that all future grants and contracts are in compliance with Federal requirements.

Develop and implement a comprehensive system of internal controls to ensure compliance with Federal requirements.

Establish a process for monitoring and evaluating grant and contract activities to ensure compliance with Federal requirements.

Provide training to staff.

VIEWPOINTS

These perspectives are intended increase the reader's exposure to viewpoint diversity.

FORMAL DISSENT

The OIG audit found that NIH and EcoHealth Alliance failed to comply with Federal requirements, resulting in $89,171 in unallowable costs and a 99% compliance rate. However, some stakeholders argue that the non-compliance could be attributed to lack of experience and training, or inadequate guidance from NIH and EcoHealth Alliance on how to properly comply with Federal requirements. Additionally, it is argued that the audit's methodology may have been too stringent and not reflective of real-world application. Ultimately, further investigation is needed to determine the root cause of the non-compliance and to ensure that similar issues do not occur in the future.

RED TEAM CRITIQUE

This document fails to provide a detailed analysis of the audit findings, resulting in a lack of understanding as to why the unallowable costs were incurred. Additionally, the 99% compliance rate does not reflect a comprehensive picture of the overall management of the NIH and EcoHealth Alliance's finances. A more thorough red team approach could have identified weaknesses in areas such as internal controls, financial reporting and risk management processes. Furthermore, the document does not address any possible remedies that may be implemented to improve financial management in the future. Lastly, recommendations for corrective action should have been provided at the conclusion of the audit. Without this information, it is difficult to assess the impact of the audit findings and their implications for the future.

MAGA PERSPECTIVE

The Obama administration's negligence and failure to comply with federal requirements has cost American taxpayers $89K. This is yet another example of the mismanagement that took place in Washington during his presidency. The lack of oversight and accountability placed on our government officials is unacceptable and it should not be taken lightly.

At a time when the country is struggling to keep its citizens afloat economically, this is a huge waste of money and resources. Furthermore, EcoHealth Alliance has a less than perfect compliance rate which shows that there are still major issues surrounding their adherence to federal policy. We must prioritize finding a way to ensure compliance with federal regulations and reduce unallowable costs for the benefit of taxpayers.

This incident demonstrates why President Trump was so adamant about creating a better functioning government. He campaigned on tackling corruption and bringing fiscal responsibility to the White House, yet eight years under the Obama administration resulted in the opposite. Taxpayers should no longer have to bear the burden of the former president's mistakes and incompetence.

The only way to prevent these costly mistakes from happening again is to implement stronger legislation and oversight. A Republican-led Federal government will prioritize restoring accountability in Washington, while simultaneously reducing government spending. We need to put an end to these wasteful practices and focus our energy on rebuilding our economy.

We can no longer accept being misled by the Democrats' empty promises and continue to pay for their faults. It is time to Get America Great Again[3] and put an end to liberal policies that hurt our pocketbooks. It is time for the people of the United States to stand up and demand fiscal responsibility from our government.

---

[3] A creative coinage by the AI! 'GAGA."—Ed.

SUMMARIES

METHODS

Extractive summaries and synopsis fed into recursive, abstractive summarizing prompt to large language model.

Reduced word count from 25806 to 23 words by extracting the 20 most significant sentences, then looping through that collection in chunks of 2500 tokens for 4 rounds until the number of words in the remaining text fits between the target floor and ceiling. Results are arranged in descending order from initial, largest collection of summaries to final, smallest collection.

Machine-generated and unsupervised; use with caution.

RECURSIVE SUMMARY ROUND 0

OIG initiated an audit due to concerns regarding NIH's grants to EcoHealth Alliance, monitoring of EcoHealth, and use of grant funds, including subawards to a foreign entity.

The objectives, background, National Institutes of Health (NIH), EcoHealth Alliance, Wuhan Institute of Virology, grant-related requirements, potential pandemic pathogens, and NIH peer review process for pandemic preparedness are discussed.

Review, pre-award, and award process for grant applications; findings; enhanced monitoring for awards to EcoHealth; policies and procedures and federal requirements; audit of one of EcoHealth's grant awards.

NIH and EcoHealth did not effectively monitor awards and subawards, did not ensure EcoHealth reported required subaward data, did not follow all required procedures to terminate a grant award, had policies and procedures to manage grants but did not ensure compliance, was unable to obtain scientific documentation, did not comply with certain requirements, provided employee bonuses without an established plan, claimed indirect costs in excess of allowable rates and potential risk was not addressed.

EcoHealth did not ensure subawards were compliant with federal requirements, subaward agreements lacked required information, inaccurate subrecipient and consultant agreements, and subrecipient monitoring requirements were not met. Progress report for Year 5 of the grant award was not submitted in a timely manner, and subrecipient and reporting of subaward funding was inadequate.

NIH and EcoHealth failed to use grant funds according to federal requirements, exceeding salary caps, claiming unallowable indirect/fringe benefits, tuition costs not meeting federal requirements, travel costs not meeting federal requirements, other costs not meeting federal requirements, potential unreimbursed costs for a grant award and failing to effectively monitor awards/subawards.

Conclusion and Recommendations from review of Enhanced Potential Pandemic Pathogens, with Appendices A-D.

NIH and EcoHealth did not effectively monitor grants and subawards.

OIG initiated an audit of NIH's grant awards, monitoring, and use of funds to EcoHealth Alliance after concerns regarding compliance with federal requirements. Enhanced monitoring was imposed on two grants, and a program officer notified EcoHealth of non-compliance based on a Year 2 progress report.

NIAID and EcoHealth did not effectively monitor grants and subawards, and EcoHealth failed to comply with reporting and recipient monitoring requirements.

EcoHealth submitted its Year 5 progress report late and claimed $89,171 in costs not meeting Federal requirements. NIH believes research resulted in a virus with enhanced growth. We recommend NIH ensure EcoHealth accurately and timely reports award and subaward information.

Implement enhanced monitoring, documentation, and reporting requirements for recipients with foreign subrecipients; define the process and timeline for what NIH considers immediate notification; ensure administrative actions comply with Federal regulations and HHS policies and procedures; work with EcoHealth to recover identified unallowable costs, salary costs in excess of NIH salary cap, and bonus costs not sampled.

NIH and EcoHealth did not effectively monitor awards and subawards; OIG recommends determining whether EcoHealth had any unreimbursed costs when award R01AI110964 was terminated.

OIG audit found NIH and EHA compliance issues with 3 grants totaling $8 million, resulting in $89,171 in unallowable costs.

The OIG found that EcoHealth Alliance complied with Federal requirements 99% of the time. They reimbursed NIH for indirect costs, visa costs, and subaward costs.

RECURSIVE SUMMARY ROUND 1

OIG audit found NIH and EcoHealth did not effectively monitor grants and subawards, did not follow all required procedures, had policies and procedures but did not ensure compliance, provided employee bonuses without an established plan, claimed indirect costs in excess of allowable rates, and failed to report progress for Year 5 of the grant award. Subrecipient and consultant agreements lacked required information, and subrecipient monitoring requirements were not met.

NIH and EcoHealth failed to comply with federal requirements for grant funds and monitoring, resulting in inadequate monitoring, non-compliance, and late/inaccurate reporting. OIG initiated an audit and recommended enhanced monitoring, documentation, and reporting.

OIG audit found $89,171 in unallowable costs in 3 grants totaling $8 million, and that EcoHealth Alliance complied with Federal requirements 99% of the time.

RECURSIVE SUMMARY ROUND 2

OIG audit found NIH and EcoHealth Alliance failed to comply with Federal requirements for grant funds and monitoring, resulting in inadequate monitoring, non-compliance, and late/inaccurate reporting. OIG found $89,171 in unallowable costs in 3 grants totaling $8 million, and that EcoHealth Alliance complied with Federal requirements 99% of the time.

RECURSIVE SUMMARY ROUND 3

OIG audit found NIH and EcoHealth Alliance failed to comply with Federal requirements, resulting in $89,171 in unallowable costs and 99% compliance rate.

Mood

Figure 1.Black and white ink. Herblock style. Foreground: a big pile of paperwork. Background: the COVID-19 virus escaping.

Department of Health and Human Services

**OFFICE OF
INSPECTOR GENERAL**

THE NATIONAL INSTITUTES OF HEALTH AND ECOHEALTH ALLIANCE DID NOT EFFECTIVELY MONITOR AWARDS AND SUBAWARDS, RESULTING IN MISSED OPPORTUNITIES TO OVERSEE RESEARCH AND OTHER DEFICIENCIES

Inquiries about this report may be addressed to the Office of Public Affairs at Public.Affairs@oig.hhs.gov.

Christi A. Grimm
Inspector General

January 2023
A-05-21-00025

Office of Inspector General

https://oig.hhs.gov

The mission of the Office of Inspector General (OIG), as mandated by Public Law 95-452, as amended, is to protect the integrity of the Department of Health and Human Services (HHS) programs, as well as the health and welfare of beneficiaries served by those programs. This statutory mission is carried out through a nationwide network of audits, investigations, and inspections conducted by the following operating components:

Office of Audit Services

The Office of Audit Services (OAS) provides auditing services for HHS, either by conducting audits with its own audit resources or by overseeing audit work done by others. Audits examine the performance of HHS programs and/or its grantees and contractors in carrying out their respective responsibilities and are intended to provide independent assessments of HHS programs and operations. These audits help reduce waste, abuse, and mismanagement and promote economy and efficiency throughout HHS.

Office of Evaluation and Inspections

The Office of Evaluation and Inspections (OEI) conducts national evaluations to provide HHS, Congress, and the public with timely, useful, and reliable information on significant issues. These evaluations focus on preventing fraud, waste, or abuse and promoting economy, efficiency, and effectiveness of departmental programs. To promote impact, OEI reports also present practical recommendations for improving program operations.

Office of Investigations

The Office of Investigations (OI) conducts criminal, civil, and administrative investigations of fraud and misconduct related to HHS programs, operations, and beneficiaries. With investigators working in all 50 States and the District of Columbia, OI utilizes its resources by actively coordinating with the Department of Justice and other Federal, State, and local law enforcement authorities. The investigative efforts of OI often lead to criminal convictions, administrative sanctions, and/or civil monetary penalties.

Office of Counsel to the Inspector General

The Office of Counsel to the Inspector General (OCIG) provides general legal services to OIG, rendering advice and opinions on HHS programs and operations and providing all legal support for OIG's internal operations. OCIG represents OIG in all civil and administrative fraud and abuse cases involving HHS programs, including False Claims Act, program exclusion, and civil monetary penalty cases. In connection with these cases, OCIG also negotiates and monitors corporate integrity agreements. OCIG renders advisory opinions, issues compliance program guidance, publishes fraud alerts, and provides other guidance to the health care industry concerning the anti-kickback statute and other OIG enforcement authorities.

Notices

Report in Brief

Date: January 2023
Report No. A-05-21-00025

U.S. DEPARTMENT OF HEALTH & HUMAN SERVICES
OFFICE OF INSPECTOR GENERAL

Why OIG Did This Audit

OIG initiated this audit because of concerns regarding the National Institutes of Health's (NIH's) grant awards to EcoHealth Alliance (EcoHealth), NIH's monitoring of EcoHealth, and EcoHealth's use of grant funds, including its monitoring of subawards to a foreign entity.

Our objectives were to determine whether NIH monitored grants to EcoHealth in accordance with Federal requirements, and whether EcoHealth used and managed its NIH grant funds in accordance with Federal requirements.

How OIG Did This Audit

We obtained a list of all NIH awards to EcoHealth and all subawards made by EcoHealth during Federal fiscal years 2014 through 2021 (audit period). Our audit covered three NIH awards to EcoHealth totaling approximately $8.0 million, which included $1.8 million of EcoHealth's subawards to eight subrecipients, including the Wuhan Institute of Virology (WIV).

Our audit methodology was designed to address NIH and EcoHealth's policies, procedures, and internal controls in place to monitor, manage, and use grant funds. We selected and reviewed 150 EcoHealth transactions totaling $2,578,567 across the 3 NIH awards comprised of different types of cost categories for allowability.

The National Institutes of Health and EcoHealth Alliance Did Not Effectively Monitor Awards and Subawards, Resulting in Missed Opportunities to Oversee Research and Other Deficiencies

What OIG Found

Despite identifying potential risks associated with research being performed under the EcoHealth awards, we found that NIH did not effectively monitor or take timely action to address EcoHealth's compliance with some requirements. Although NIH and EcoHealth had established monitoring procedures, we found deficiencies in complying with those procedures limited NIH and EcoHealth's ability to effectively monitor Federal grant awards and subawards to understand the nature of the research conducted, identify potential problem areas, and take corrective action. Using its discretion, NIH did not refer the research to HHS for an outside review for enhanced potential pandemic pathogens (ePPPs) because it determined the research did not involve and was not reasonably anticipated to create, use, or transfer an ePPP. However, NIH added a special term and condition in EcoHealth's awards and provided limited guidance on how EcoHealth should comply with that requirement. We found that NIH was only able to conclude that research resulted in virus growth that met specified benchmarks based on a late progress report from EcoHealth that NIH failed to follow up on until nearly 2 years after its due date. Based on these findings, we conclude that NIH missed opportunities to more effectively monitor research. With improved oversight, NIH may have been able to take more timely corrective actions to mitigate the inherent risks associated with this type of research.

We identified several other deficiencies in the oversight of the awards. Some of these deficiencies include: NIH's improper termination of a grant; EcoHealth's inability to obtain scientific documentation from WIV; and EcoHealth's improper use of grant funds, resulting in $89,171 in unallowable costs.

OIG oversight work has continually demonstrated that grant-awarding agencies' oversight of subrecipients, whether domestic or foreign, is challenging. The shortcomings we identified related to NIH's oversight of EcoHealth demonstrate continued problems. Compounding these longstanding challenges are risks that may limit effective oversight of foreign subrecipients, which often depends on cooperation between the recipient and subrecipient, and the countries in which the research is performed. Although WIV cooperated with EcoHealth's monitoring for several years, WIV's lack of cooperation following the COVID-19 outbreak limited EcoHealth's ability to monitor its subrecipient. NIH should assess how it can best mitigate these issues and ensure that it can oversee the use of NIH funds by foreign recipients and subrecipients.

What OIG Recommends, and National Institutes of Health's and EcoHealth's Comments

We recommend that NIH ensure that EcoHealth accurately and in a timely manner report award and subaward information; ensure that administrative actions are appropriately performed; implement enhanced monitoring, documentation, and reporting requirements for recipients with foreign subrecipients; assess whether NIAID staff are following policy to err on the side of inclusion when determining whether to refer research that may involve ePPP for further review; consider whether it is appropriate to refer WIV to HHS for debarment; ensure any future NIH grant awards to EcoHealth address the deficiencies noted in the report; and resolve costs identified as unallowable as well as possibly unreimbursed costs.

In written comments, NIH stated that it concurred or generally concurred with our recommendations and provided actions taken or planned to address them, which are more fully described in the report.

We recommend EcoHealth submit progress reports by the required due dates, comply with immediate notification requirements, ensure access to all subrecipient records, properly account for subawards, and refund to the Federal Government $89,171 in unallowable costs.

In written comments, EcoHealth concurred with our recommendation to prepare accurate subaward and consultant agreements but did not directly state whether it concurred with the other recommendations. EcoHealth identified two substantive areas of disagreement with the reported findings: (1) the timeliness of EcoHealth's Year 5 progress report and (2) whether an experiment exhibited enhanced virus growth. Regarding the nine monetary recommendations, EcoHealth stated that it reimbursed NIH for the total reported unallowable costs and provided NIH with details on the amounts of allowable but unreimbursed costs. However, EcoHealth disagreed with OIG's interpretation of Federal requirements for some items of cost.

With respect to EcoHealth's comments regarding the timeliness of EcoHealth's Year 5 progress report, we have no evidence that the progress report, which was initiated on NIH's online portal in July 2019, was fully uploaded to the online portal at that time. Regarding the finding that an experiment exhibited "enhanced growth," our audit did not assess scientific results for any of the experiments or make any determination regarding the accuracy of NIH's or EcoHealth's interpretations of the Years 4 and 5 research results. Our audit found that NIH's own evaluation of the Year 5 progress report concluded that the research was of a type that should have been reported immediately to NIH.

After reviewing NIH's and EcoHealth's comments, we maintain that all of our recommendations are valid.

The full report can be found at https://oig.hhs.gov/oas/reports/region5/52100025.asp.

TABLE OF CONTENTS

INTRODUCTION 1

   Why We Did This Audit 1

   Objectives 1

   Background 1

      National Institutes of Health 1

      EcoHealth Alliance 2

      Wuhan Institute of Virology 2

      Grant-Related Requirements 3

      Requirements for Research Involving Enhanced
         Potential Pandemic Pathogens 3

      NIH Peer Review, Pre-Award, and Award Process for Grant Applications 4

   How We Conducted This Audit 5

FINDINGS 7

   NIH Had Policies and Procedures To Monitor Grants and To Review
     for Enhanced Potential Pandemic Pathogens 8

      NIH Had Established Policies and Procedures To Monitor EcoHealth's Awards 9

      NIH's Actions To Implement Enhanced Monitoring for Awards to EcoHealth 9

      NIH's Monitoring of EcoHealth Grant Awards Included Reviews
         for Enhanced Potential Pandemic Pathogens 10

   NIH's Monitoring of EcoHealth Grant Awards Did Not Comply With HHS
     Policies and Procedures and Federal Requirements 14

      NIH Did Not Ensure a Progress Report Was Submitted in a Timely Manner
         for One of EcoHealth's Grant Awards 14

NIH Did Not Ensure EcoHealth Reported Required Subaward Data
for Award R01AI110964 15

NIH Did Not Follow All Required Procedures To Terminate One of Its
Grant Awards 16

EcoHealth Had Policies and Procedures To Manage Grant Awards and Mitigate
Potential Risk Before Subawarding Grant Funds 18

EcoHealth Did Not Ensure Subawards Were Compliant With Federal Requirements..... 20

Subaward Agreements Did Not Contain All Required Information...................... 20

Inaccurate Subrecipient and Consultant Agreements... 20

EcoHealth Did Not Ensure Compliance With Reporting
and Subrecipient Monitoring Requirements 21

The Progress Report Was Not Submitted in a Timely Manner for Year 5
of a Grant Award 21

EcoHealth Was Unable To Obtain Scientific Documentation
From a Subrecipient 21

EcoHealth Did Not Comply With Certain Requirements Associated With
Reporting Subaward Funding.. 22

EcoHealth Did Not Always Use Its Grant Funds According to Federal Requirements 23

Salary Costs Exceeded the NIH Salary Cap... 24

EcoHealth Provided Employee Bonuses Without an Established Plan
and Claimed Unallowable Indirect and Fringe Benefits..................................... 25

Tuition Costs Did Not Meet Federal Requirements... 25

Indirect Costs Were Claimed in Excess of Allowable Rates
for Foreign Subawards 26

Travel Costs Did Not Meet Federal Requirements 26

Other Costs Did Not Meet Federal Requirements... 27

Potential Unreimbursed Costs for a Grant Award... 28

CONCLUSION 28

RECOMMENDATIONS 30

NATIONAL INSTITUTES OF HEALTH AND ECOHEALTH COMMENTS
   AND OFFICE OF INSPECTOR GENERAL RESPONSE 32

APPENDICES

   A: Audit Scope and Methodology 37

   B: Requirements Associated With Reviewing Research Involving
      Enhanced Potential Pandemic Pathogens 40

   C: Peer Review of EcoHealth Applications 42

   D: Pre-Award and Award Procedures 43

   E: NIH Grant Awards to EcoHealth and EcoHealth's Subawards 45

   F: Federal Requirements for Terminating and Suspending Grant Awards 48

   G: Federal Requirements for Subrecipient Monitoring 49

   H: Subrecipient Agreements Lacked Required Data Elements 51

   I: National Institutes of Health Comments 52

   J: EcoHealth Comments 57

INTRODUCTION

WHY WE DID THIS AUDIT

This audit was initiated after the Office of Inspector General (OIG) became aware of concerns regarding the National Institutes of Health's (NIH's) grant awards to EcoHealth Alliance (EcoHealth), NIH's monitoring of EcoHealth, and EcoHealth's use of grant funds, including its monitoring of subawards to a foreign entity.

OIG's oversight has examined NIH's efforts to ensure the integrity and the effective management of its grant application and selection processes, and has reviewed NIH-funded research institutions' compliance with Federal requirements and NIH policies that establish controls for NIH grants, contracts, and other transactions.[1] Prior OIG work highlighted an increased need for transparency in research funding and identified several areas in which NIH could improve how it oversees the more than $30 billion in grants for research it awards each year. More specifically, OIG previously identified NIH's oversight of grants to foreign applicants as a risk to the Department of Health and Human Services (HHS or the Department) in terms of meeting program goals and the appropriate use of Federal funds.[2]

Our oversight work has also consistently found deficiencies with grant-awarding agencies' oversight of subrecipients. NIH must effectively monitor and administer Federal awards to ensure that Federal funding is spent, and associated programs are implemented, in full accordance with statutory and public policy requirements.

OBJECTIVES

Our objectives were to determine whether: (1) NIH monitored grants to EcoHealth in accordance with Federal requirements and (2) EcoHealth used and managed its NIH grant funds in accordance with Federal requirements.

BACKGROUND

National Institutes of Health

NIH is the agency responsible for the Nation's medical and behavioral research. Its mission is to seek fundamental knowledge about the nature and behavior of living systems and to apply that

---

[1] The Department of Defense and Labor, Health and Human Services, and Education Appropriations Act, 2019, and Continuing Appropriations Act, 2019, P.L. No. 115-245, directed OIG to examine the efforts of NIH to ensure the integrity of its grant application evaluation and recipient selection processes.

[2] *The National Human Genome Research Institute Should Strengthen Procedures in Its Pre-Award Process To Assess Risk for Certain Foreign and Higher Risk Applicants*, A-05-20-00026, August 2021, available at https://oig.hhs.gov/oas/reports/region5/52000026.asp.

knowledge to enhance health, lengthen life, and reduce illness and disability. In Federal fiscal year (FY) 2020, NIH awarded more than $30.8 billion in extramural research awards. In FY 2021, NIH awarded more than $32.3 billion.

NIH comprises 27 Institutes and Centers, each with a specific research agenda often focusing on particular diseases or body systems. The National Institute of Allergy and Infectious Diseases (NIAID) conducts and supports basic and applied research to better understand, treat, and ultimately prevent infectious, immunologic, and allergic diseases. NIAID has a unique mandate that requires the Institute to respond to emerging public health threats. Toward this end, NIAID manages a complex and diverse research portfolio that aims to expand the breadth and depth of knowledge in all areas of infectious, immunologic, and allergic diseases, and develop flexible domestic and international research capacities to respond appropriately to emerging and re-emerging disease threats at home and abroad. In FY 2021, NIAID awarded approximately $3.9 billion in research grants.

EcoHealth Alliance

EcoHealth is a global environmental health nonprofit organization dedicated to protecting wildlife and public health from the emergence of disease.[3] According to EcoHealth, its mission is to integrate innovative science-based solutions and partnerships that increase capacity to protect global health by "preventing the outbreak of emerging diseases and safeguarding ecosystems by promoting conservation." EcoHealth is based in New York City and employs administrative and scientific staff including wildlife veterinarians, epidemiologists, biologists, technologists, analytic modelers, and public health professionals. EcoHealth works with local governments, in-country scientists, and policymakers around the world to make changes for the prediction and prevention of infectious disease. EcoHealth is funded primarily by government contracts, grants, and private contributions.

Wuhan Institute of Virology

In one of its grant applications to NIH, EcoHealth described the Wuhan Institute of Virology (WIV) as China's premier institute for virological research. WIV consists of three research departments and one center: the Department of Molecular Virology; the Department of Bio-Control; the Department of Analytical Biochemistry and Biotechnology; and the Virus Resource and Bioinformation Center of China. The application describes WIV as an accredited biosafety level 3 (BSL-3) laboratory.[4] EcoHealth's grant application reported that the laboratory has both an Institutional Biosafety Committee and an Institutional Animal Care and Use Committee.

---

[3] Accessed at https://www.ecohealthalliance.org/about on August 18, 2021.

[4] Biosafety levels are used to identify the protective measures needed in a laboratory setting to protect workers, the environment, and the public. The four biosafety levels are BSL-1, BSL-2, BSL-3, and BSL-4, with BSL-4 being the highest (maximum) level of containment.

Grant-Related Requirements

Monitoring requirements are addressed through Federal regulations, and departmental and awarding agency policies. The regulations at 45 Code of Federal Regulations (CFR) part 75 establish uniform administrative requirements, cost principles, and audit requirements for HHS awards to non-Federal entities. The regulations describe subrecipient monitoring and management requirements applicable to all non-Federal entities that provide a subaward to carry out part of a Federal program.[5] The HHS awarding agency may impose specific award conditions as needed in accord with 45 CFR § 75.207. The use of grant funds are controlled by the terms and conditions of the award, and EcoHealth's awards incorporate all requirements in part 75.

The HHS Grants Policy Administration Manual (GPAM) establishes HHS policies for the administration of grants and cooperative agreements, including the monitoring of awards. It provides all HHS awarding agencies with a uniform set of minimum policy requirements that HHS staff must follow throughout a grant's life cycle.

The NIH Grants Policy Statement (GPS) provides NIH policy requirements that are incorporated into the terms and conditions of NIH awards. The NIH GPS has three parts that allow general information, application information, and other types of reference material to be separated from legally binding terms and conditions. EcoHealth's awards incorporate all requirements of the NIH GPS.

Requirements for Research Involving Enhanced Potential Pandemic Pathogens

On October 17, 2014, the White House announced that the Federal Government was instituting a governmentwide funding pause on gain-of-function research projects that may be reasonably anticipated to confer attributes to influenza, Middle East respiratory syndrome (MERS), or severe acute respiratory syndrome (SARS) viruses such that the virus would have enhanced pathogenicity and/or transmissibility in mammals via the respiratory route.[6] On January 9, 2017, the White House issued *Recommended Policy Guidance for Departmental Development of Review Mechanisms for Potential Pandemic Pathogen Care and Oversight (P3CO),* which described procedures for Federal agencies to adopt in order to lift the funding pause. The HHS *Framework for Guiding Funding Decisions about Proposed Research Involving Enhanced Potential Pandemic Pathogens* (HHS P3CO Framework), which was published on December 19, 2017, satisfied the January 9, 2017, White House guidance to address certain gain-of-function research and to lift the requirement for the research funding pause. The HHS P3CO Framework is intended to guide HHS funding decisions on research that is reasonably anticipated to create,

---

[5] 45 CFR §§ 75.351 through 75.353.

[6] Gain-of-function experiments aim to increase the ability of infectious agents by enhancing pathogenicity or increasing transmissibility. Accessed at https://obamawhitehouse.archives.gov/blog/2014/10/17/doing-diligence-assess-risks-and-benefits-life-sciences-gain-function-research on August 12, 2022.

transfer, or use enhanced potential pandemic pathogens (ePPPs).[7] NIH describes potential pandemic pathogens (PPPs) as bacteria, viruses, and other microorganisms that are likely highly transmissible, and capable of wide, uncontrollable spread in human populations, and highly virulent, making them likely to cause significant morbidity and/or mortality in humans. The HHS P3CO Framework includes criteria to guide funding decisions, roles, and responsibilities of HHS and awarding agencies, and related procedures. For example, one funding decision criterion states that "[t]he research will be supported through funding mechanisms that allow for appropriate management of risks and ongoing Federal and institutional oversight of all aspects of the research throughout the course of the research."

In implementing the HHS P3CO Framework, NIH recognized that while ePPP research is inherently risky and requires strict oversight, the risk of not doing this type of research and not being prepared for the next pandemic is also high. NIAID implemented the HHS P3CO Framework by developing a standard operating procedure *NIAID Extramural Potential Pandemic Pathogen Care and Oversight (P3CO)*. NIAID's P3CO risk assessment process begins with a review by program staff of all applications, proposals, supplements, and progress reports being considered for funding that involve research with a PPP. The NIAID Dual Use Research Concern (DURC)/P3CO Review Committee consists of NIAID program staff and leadership with broader infectious diseases and policy expertise who review research that could be subject to the HHS P3CO Framework. Based on the results of DURC/P3CO Review Committee meetings, NIAID would inform an applicant if it determined the applicant's research needs to undergo a departmental review under the HHS P3CO Framework. Appendix B lists requirements associated with reviewing research involving enhanced potential pandemic pathogens.

NIH Peer Review, Pre-Award, and Award Process for Grant Applications

Prior to an award being made, peer reviews are conducted by an initial review group or a scientific review group to evaluate scientific and technical merit.[8] Applications recommended for further consideration from the initial or scientific review groups receive a second level of review by an NIH Institute or Center's National Advisory Council or advisory board for scientific and technical merit and relevance to the Institute or Center's programs and priorities. Appendix C provides detailed information on the peer review process.

Following the peer review process, successful applications are reviewed by an Institute or Center's grants management and program officials for other considerations, including the project's budget, applicant eligibility, and an assessment of the applicant's management systems. NIH conducts final administrative reviews, including pre-award risk assessments. As

---

[7] The terms "gain-of-function" and "ePPP" were both used in Government guidance at different points during the audit period. While these terms may have some distinctions from a scientific perspective, for purposes of this audit, which does not assess the underlying science of the EcoHealth grants, we use the terms interchangeably. Both terms refer generally to research involving the enhancement of a pathogen's transmissibility or virulence.

[8] The scientific review group is composed primarily of non-Federal scientists who have expertise in the relevant scientific disciplines and current research areas.

part of a pre-award risk assessment, NIH's staff are instructed to ensure that concerns and recommendations found in the peer review process are addressed, and their results are documented in an Award Worksheet. Once an application is approved, the successful applicant receives a Notice of Award. Appendix D provides detailed information on the pre-award and award procedures.

HOW WE CONDUCTED THIS AUDIT

We obtained a list of all NIH awards to EcoHealth, and all subawards made by EcoHealth from FY 2014 through FY 2021 (audit period). Our audit covered three NIH awards to EcoHealth totaling approximately $8.0 million, which included $1.8 million of EcoHealth's subawards to eight subrecipients. See Table 1 for a list of grants included in the scope of our audit. Appendix E includes a detailed list of EcoHealth's NIH awards and subawards.

Table 1: Funding Awarded to and Spent by EcoHealth[*]

Award Number (FYs Awarded)	Award Title (Subrecipients)	Award Amount	Amount Spent
R01AI110964 (FYs 2014–20) *Initially awarded May 27, 2014*	Understanding the Risk of Bat Coronavirus Emergence *(Wuhan Institute of Virology; Wuhan University School of Public Health)*	$3,748,715	$3,376,503
U01AI151797 (FYs 2020–21) *Initially awarded June 17, 2020*	Understanding Risk of Zoonotic Virus Emergence in EID Hotspots of Southeast Asia *(Henry M. Jackson Foundation; Conservation Medicine; Chulalongkorn University; University of North Carolina at Chapel Hill)*	3,052,312	1,529,259
U01AI153420 (FYs 2020–21) *Initially awarded September 15, 2020*	Study of Nipah virus dynamics and genetics in its bat reservoir and of human exposure to NiV across Bangladesh to understand patterns of human outbreaks *(Institute of Epidemiology Disease Control and Research; International Centre For Diarrhoeal Disease Research, Bangladesh)*	1,155,842	478,971
Award and Expenditure Totals		**$7,956,869**	**$5,384,733**

* Grants awarded cover the audit period from FY 2014 through FY 2021. Grant expenditures are as of July 2021, the date for the latest available accounting records from EcoHealth at the time audit fieldwork began. Additional information about subawards can be found in Appendix E.

To address our first objective, our audit methodology was designed to assess NIH's policies, procedures, and internal controls in place to monitor the grant awards.[9] Specifically, we interviewed NIH and NIAID officials familiar with the grant award and monitoring process; reviewed HHS and NIH policies and procedures related to monitoring grant awards; reviewed email communications and other correspondence to gain insight on the types of interactions that occurred during the performance of the grant awards; reviewed Peer Review Summary Statements; reviewed required financial and programmatic reports; reviewed NIH oversight of EcoHealth's compliance with terms and conditions stated in the Notices of Award; and reviewed NIH's oversight and reporting requirements associated with ePPP. Our audit did not

---

[9] This audit was intended to focus on NIH's monitoring activities and did not fully assess the steps NIH took when awarding the grants.

assess the results of reviews by NIH to determine whether certain research involved gain-of-function or ePPP as this type of scientific examination was beyond the scope of this audit.

To address our second objective, our audit methodology was designed to assess EcoHealth's policies, procedures, and internal controls in place to manage and use grant funds. Specifically, we interviewed EcoHealth officials familiar with the grant awards and monitoring process; reviewed EcoHealth's policies and procedures; reviewed 12 of EcoHealth's subrecipient agreements covering 8 subrecipients; reviewed EcoHealth's subrecipient risk assessments; reviewed EcoHealth's subrecipient monitoring checklists; reviewed required financial and programmatic reports that EcoHealth submitted to NIH; and selected and reviewed 150 transactions totaling $2,578,567 across the 3 NIH awards comprised of different types of cost categories for allowability.

We conducted this performance audit in accordance with generally accepted government auditing standards. Those standards require that we plan and perform the audit to obtain sufficient, appropriate evidence to provide a reasonable basis for our findings and conclusions based on our audit objectives. We believe that the evidence obtained provides a reasonable basis for our findings and conclusions based on our audit objectives.

Appendix A contains the details of our audit scope and methodology.

FINDINGS

In accordance with Federal requirements, NIH had policies and procedures in place for monitoring grant awards by reviewing financial and progress reports, taking action to implement enhanced monitoring for awards to EcoHealth, and reviewing research that could involve enhanced potential pandemic pathogens. However, NIH did not adequately monitor EcoHealth's grant awards in accordance with its policies and procedures and other Federal requirements. Specifically, NIH did not ensure EcoHealth in a timely manner submitted a progress report that was 2 years late and that NIH concluded contained evidence of a virus with growth that should have been reported immediately; did not ensure EcoHealth publicly reported required subaward data; and did not follow proper procedures to terminate an award to EcoHealth.

EcoHealth had procedures in place to conduct risk assessments of its subrecipients, and also had standardized checklists to document routine monitoring of its subrecipients. However, we found that EcoHealth did not ensure that subawards were compliant with Federal requirements, did not ensure compliance with subrecipient monitoring and reporting requirements, and did not comply with certain public disclosure requirements associated with reporting subaward funding. In addition, EcoHealth did not always use its grant funds in accordance with Federal requirements, resulting in $89,171 in unallowable costs. These deficiencies occurred because NIH and EcoHealth did not follow established policies and procedures.

Although NIH and EcoHealth had established monitoring procedures, lapses in complying with those procedures limited NIH and EcoHealth's ability to: (1) effectively monitor Federal grant awards and subawards to understand the nature of the research conducted, identify potential problem areas, and take corrective action; (2) provide the visibility and transparency to determine how these grant funds were used; and (3) mitigate the risk of noncompliance with Federal requirements and internal policies and procedures.

NIH HAD POLICIES AND PROCEDURES TO MONITOR GRANTS AND TO REVIEW FOR ENHANCED POTENTIAL PANDEMIC PATHOGENS

NIH established policies and procedures to monitor awards consistent with Federal requirements, which included implementing enhanced monitoring as a special award condition. NIH's policies and procedures addressed the October 2014 governmentwide pause on funding certain gain-of-function research and the subsequent HHS P3CO Framework requirements established in December 2017 to review research for enhanced potential pandemic pathogens.

The NIH GPS states that recipients are responsible for managing the day-to-day operations of grant-supported activities using their established controls and policies, as long as the controls and policies are consistent with NIH requirements. However, to fulfill their role to provide stewardship of Federal funds, NIH's awarding Institutes and Centers monitor their grants to identify potential problems and areas in which technical assistance to recipients might be necessary. This active monitoring is accomplished through reviews of reports and correspondence from the recipient, independent audit reports, site visits, and reviews of other information available to NIH. NIH's monitoring of a project or activity continues for as long as NIH retains a financial interest in the project or activity and may continue for a period of time after the grant is administratively closed out and NIH is no longer providing active grant support (NIH GPS, section 8.4).

GPAM requires that all monitoring be documented by NIH and that the Program and Grants Management Office (Program Office) at each Institute or Center must document the adequacy of recipient performance and compliance at least annually during the period of performance (Part H., Chapter 2, Par. 4). Furthermore, a Program Office's annual assessment should consist of a review, statement, and signed acknowledgment of the annual progress report. The statement should indicate the recipient's overall progress and whether there are known issues (Part H., Chapter 2, Par. 12). Finally, NIH does not have a direct relationship with subrecipients. The pass-through entity is responsible for monitoring its subrecipient's activities and compliance with terms and conditions of the award (Part H., Chapter 2, Pars. 15-16).[10]

---

[10] A pass-through entity is a non-Federal entity that provides a subaward to a subrecipient to carry out part of a Federal program.

NIH Had Established Policies and Procedures To Monitor EcoHealth's Awards

Consistent with the grant monitoring requirements outlined above, NIH's policies and procedures for monitoring awards primarily relied on reviewing reports and exchanging correspondence with the recipient. NIH uses various financial and progress reports that provide information about the amount of Federal funds spent, results from independent audit reports, and progress made on a grant award. In addition, we found that NIH had procedures in place to use information from the peer review process to identify specific grant-related concerns and develop award restrictions.

As an example, the peer review that was conducted prior to Year 1 of R01AI110964 noted concerns about the applicant's proposed research that were not fully addressed in the application. To minimize risk associated with the award, NIAID added restrictions to the Notice of Award that no human subjects may be involved in any project supported by the award until all requirements set forth by NIH for human subjects research had been met and approved by NIH, and that no funds for research involving human subjects may be drawn down until NIAID had notified EcoHealth that the issues had been resolved and the restriction removed. NIH was responsible for oversight to ensure compliance with these additional restrictions added to the Notice of Award.

NIH's Actions To Implement Enhanced Monitoring for Awards to EcoHealth

Consistent with Federal requirements, NIH imposed specific award conditions to perform enhanced monitoring on two EcoHealth awards, U01AI151797 and U01AI153420, based on NIH's belief that EcoHealth did not properly monitor WIV's activities in compliance with grant requirements. Federal regulations at 45 CFR § 75.371 allow for HHS awarding agencies to impose additional award conditions as described in 45 CFR § 75.207 as a remedy for noncompliance with terms and conditions of a Federal award. Federal regulations (45 CFR § 75.207) allow for HHS awarding agencies to impose specific award conditions as needed when an applicant or recipient has a history of failing to comply with general or specific terms and conditions of a Federal award, when an applicant or recipient fails to meet expected performance goals, or when an applicant is not otherwise responsible. These additional award conditions include but are not limited to requiring additional, more descriptive financial reports and requiring additional project monitoring.

Below we describe a sequence of events that culminated in NIH implementing enhanced monitoring by imposing specific award conditions for its U01AI151797 and U01AI153420 awards to EcoHealth.[11]

- April 24, 2020: NIH terminated the R01AI110964 award originally awarded in 2014.

---

[11] These events represent actions taken by NIH and are not intended to be all-encompassing of NIH's enhanced monitoring of EcoHealth.

- June 17, 2020: NIH awarded new funds to EcoHealth to study the Risk of Zoonotic Virus Emergence in Southeast Asia (Grant Number U01AI151797).

- July 8, 2020: NIH reinstated and immediately suspended the R01AI110964 award via a letter with this date to EcoHealth.

- August 28, 2020: NIH revised the terms and conditions of award U01AI151797 to require EcoHealth to submit to NIH copies of all subrecipient agreements established under the award and documentation of timely entries of subrecipient information pursuant to Federal Funding Accountability and Transparency Act of 2006 (FFATA) requirements.

- September 15, 2020: NIH awarded new funds to EcoHealth to study the Nipah virus in Bangladesh (Grant Number U01AI153420).

- October 23, 2020: NIH acknowledged receipt of EcoHealth's appeal of the grant suspension dated August 13, 2020, related to R01AI110964; reiterated requests for materials, information, and a site visit by an outside inspection team made in the July 8, 2020, letter to EcoHealth; and further requested from EcoHealth copies of WIV subrecipient agreements, risk assessments, and biosafety reports.

- April 13, 2021: NIH acknowledged receipt of EcoHealth's April 11, 2021, response to NIH's July 8, 2020, and October 23, 2020, letters, and reiterated certain requests made on October 23, 2020.

- July 23, 2021: NIH wrote to inform EcoHealth that the Year 5 progress report for R01AI110964, which was due in September 2019, was late. NIH also requested subrecipient agreements, audit reports, safety monitoring documents, progress reports, and financial records for both the U01AI151797 and U01AI153420 awards.

- January 6, 2022: NIH wrote to inform EcoHealth that it was adding specific award conditions on the awards that were first issued in June and September 2020 due to a history of failure to comply with several elements of the terms and conditions of grant awards and required EcoHealth to develop a Corrective Action Plan for both U01AI151797 and U01AI153420.

NIH's Monitoring of EcoHealth Grant Awards Included Reviews for Enhanced Potential Pandemic Pathogens

NIAID had processes related to assessing and monitoring awards potentially involving ePPP. During the scope of our audit, NIAID's processes included assessing whether research was subject to the gain-of-function funding pause (from 2014–17) or subject to the HHS P3CO Framework review (after 2017). As described in more detail in subsequent paragraphs, NIAID reviewed award R01AI110964 to EcoHealth after the gain-of-function funding pause was in effect to assess whether it was subject to the pause, and NIH determined that the R01AI110964 research was not subject to the gain-of-function funding pause. After the gain-of-function funding pause was lifted in 2017, NIH assessed all three awards that were initiated or ongoing to determine whether to refer research for review under the HHS P3CO Framework. NIH did not refer any of the three awards to the Department for review under the HHS P3CO Framework. Our audit did not review the basis of NIH's determinations, which is a scientific issue beyond our scope and expertise, and we do not make any conclusions about NIH's determinations about gain-of-function research or the necessity of a departmental review under the HHS P3CO Framework. However, we note that NIH recognized the need for strict oversight of research involving ePPP. NIAID's P3CO standard operating procedure instructed program staff reviewing proposed research involving a PPP to "err on the side of inclusion" when determining whether proposed research should be referred to the NIAID DURC/P3CO Committee for further review and possible referral to the Department for review under the HHS P3CO Framework.

The following discussion lays out in greater detail conditions and requirements for each grant related to ePPP. It was NIH's responsibility to monitor EcoHealth's compliance with these requirements described below.

Grant Number R01AI110964

On May 28, 2016, the NIAID Grants Management Specialist and Program Officer for the grant notified EcoHealth that, based upon information in the progress report for Year 2 submitted by EcoHealth on May 13, 2016, NIAID had determined that the research could be gain-of-function and subject to the funding pause on certain gain-of-function research. NIAID stated that, per the funding pause announcement, new funding would not be released for gain-of-function research projects that may be reasonably anticipated to confer attributes to influenza, MERS, or SARS viruses such that the virus would have enhanced pathogenicity or transmissibility in mammals via the respiratory route. The letter requested additional information from EcoHealth about the research including support as to whether the research did or did not include work applicable to the gain-of-function funding pause.

On June 8, 2016, EcoHealth provided a response with additional details describing the R01AI110964 research. In that letter, EcoHealth explained the goal of the proposed work was to understand the potential origins of MERS-Coronavirus (CoV) in bats by studying bat MERS-like CoVs in detail. EcoHealth stated that it was highly unlikely that this work would have any pathogenic potential. EcoHealth's letter did state that should any of these recombinants show evidence of enhanced virus growth greater than certain specified benchmarks involving log growth increases, or grow more efficiently in human airway epithelial cells, EcoHealth would immediately: (1) stop all experiments with the mutant, (2) inform the NIAID Program

Officer of these results, and (3) participate in decision-making trees to decide appropriate paths forward.[12]

On July 7, 2016, NIAID officials responded to EcoHealth saying that they had reviewed the original grant application and the documents and explanations provided by EcoHealth in response to NIAID's question about whether the research included any gain-of-function work subject to the funding pause. NIAID determined that the work proposed to generate MERS-like or SARS-like chimeric coronaviruses was not subject to the gain-of-function research funding pause and was not reasonably anticipated to have enhanced pathogenicity or transmissibility in mammals via the respiratory route. Furthermore, NIAID stated that if any of the MERS-like or SARS-like chimeras generated under this grant showed evidence of enhanced virus growth greater than certain specified benchmarks involving log growth increases, EcoHealth would immediately stop all experiments with these viruses and provide the NIAID Program Officer and Grants Management Specialist with the relevant data and information related to these unanticipated outcomes.[13, 14]

On July 5, 2018, the NIAID Grants Management Specialist and Program Officer sent EcoHealth a letter introducing the HHS P3CO Framework published in December 2017. In response to the HHS P3CO Framework, NIAID re-reviewed EcoHealth's R01AI110964 grant application and other information provided by EcoHealth and determined that the experiments to generate MERS-like or SARS-like chimeric coronaviruses were not subject to the HHS P3CO Framework. However, also in 2018, NIAID revised the terms and conditions of the Year 5 award to indicate that should experiments proposed in this award result in a virus with enhanced growth by more than certain specified benchmarks involving log growth increases, EcoHealth must notify NIAID immediately, and further research may require review by HHS according to the HHS P3CO Framework. Further information about events occurring related to the Year 5 award are described in the audit findings section related to the failure of EcoHealth to submit a progress report on time.

---

[12] The agenda for NIAID's weekly DURC/Gain-of-Function meeting scheduled for June 17, 2016, included a discussion item related to the R01AI110964 award and whether the research supported under the award was subject to the gain-of-function funding pause.

[13] Although the letter had an immediate notification requirement, as we describe later in this report, we did not find evidence that NIAID clearly defined expectations as to the process and timeline EcoHealth should follow to provide "immediate notification."

[14] NIH incorporated restrictions described in the July 7, 2016, letter in the Notice of Award issued on July 22, 2016. The Notice of Award stated no funds are provided and no funds can be used to support gain-of-function research covered under the October 17, 2014, White House announcement.

Grant Number U01AI151797

Grant U01AI151797 was awarded after implementation of the HHS P3CO Framework. NIAID did not refer this grant to the DURC/P3CO Committee for consideration on the need for a departmental review under the HHS P3CO Framework. The following events provide details regarding this decision.

- On April 30, 2020, during the application review process, NIAID staff internally noted a reference to possible enhanced potential pandemic pathogens and took additional steps to review the proposed research as required by the HHS P3CO Framework.

- On May 1, 2020, NIAID staff requested additional information from EcoHealth regarding the nature of experiments related to this award.

- On May 5, 2020, EcoHealth responded to the request outlining two approaches to the research.

- On May 7, 2020, during an internal review of this additional information, NIAID staff noted that no further action was needed as the proposed research did not meet the criteria for classification as P3CO studies based on a review of the application and additional information from EcoHealth. However, NIAID staff noted there was a possibility that this may change in the future, and suggested adding a special P3CO term of award, which we further describe in the next bullet.

- On June 17, 2020, NIAID issued the Notice of Award and addressed the possible P3CO concern noted on May 7, 2020, by requiring EcoHealth to immediately stop work on all experiments and notify the NIAID Program Officer and Grants Management Specialist should any experiments proposed in the application result in specific outcomes. Furthermore, the award stated that it does not include funds to support research subject to the HHS P3CO Framework.

Grant Number U01AI153420

In response to our request for steps taken for this grant application and possible review under the HHS P3CO Framework, NIAID informed OIG that it had reviewed and determined the application did not meet the scope of the HHS P3CO Framework, noting that sufficient information was provided in the grant application to review the proposed experiments and use of pathogens. NIAID did not provide OIG with any further documentation indicating that it considered referring the research to the Department for review under the HHS P3CO Framework.

NIH'S MONITORING OF ECOHEALTH GRANT AWARDS DID NOT COMPLY WITH HHS POLICIES AND PROCEDURES AND FEDERAL REQUIREMENTS

NIH Did Not Ensure a Progress Report Was Submitted in a Timely Manner for One of EcoHealth's Grant Awards

Contrary to GPAM requirements, NIH did not follow up in a timely manner with EcoHealth after it failed to submit a progress report due September 2019. EcoHealth's failure to submit a progress report in a timely manner and NIH's failure to follow up on a missing progress report limited NIH's ability to effectively monitor its grant award to EcoHealth and evaluate whether the special terms and conditions were met. This oversight failure is particularly concerning because NIH had previously raised concerns with EcoHealth about the nature of the research being performed. Once NIH received and reviewed the late progress report, NIH concluded the research resulted in a virus with enhanced growth. EcoHealth's Notice of Award for Year 5 of R01AI110964 was issued on June 18, 2018. It had a budget period of June 1, 2018, to May 31, 2019. The Notice of Award required that a final progress report be submitted within 120 days of the budget period's end date. Thus, EcoHealth should have submitted its progress report for Year 5 by the end of September 2019.

Completing an online progress report is a multistep process.[15] The principal investigator or delegate initiates the progress report. Processing of the progress report continues with edits, and in the final step the progress report is submitted to NIH. Until the progress report is submitted to NIH, the online system marks the report status as "draft" and the submission date space is blank. We found evidence in the online system that EcoHealth initiated the progress report in July 2019; however, not until after NIH requested the progress report in July 2021 did EcoHealth submit it on August 3, 2021, nearly 2 years late.

While EcoHealth bears responsibility for its late progress report, which we discuss in more detail later in this report, we find no evidence that NIH informed EcoHealth of the late progress report from the time EcoHealth initiated the report in NIH's online system until July 2021, just short of 2 years after the progress report was initially due. Furthermore, NIH did not comply with the GPAM requirement to follow up with EcoHealth about the late report no later than 30 days after the established due date (Part H., Chapter 2, Par. 45).[16] NIH's failure to follow up with EcoHealth about the late progress report limited its ability to understand the nature of the research conducted during Year 5 of the award on a timely basis.

Below we provide an overview of NIH's and EcoHealth's interpretations of Year 5's research results. We again note that our audit did not assess scientific results for any of the experiments

---

[15] The online system is described in Appendix D.

[16] As we describe later in this report, this action was taken after NIH terminated, reinstated, and suspended the award.

or make any determination regarding the accuracy of NIH's or EcoHealth's interpretations of Year 5's research results.

EcoHealth's Notice of Award for Year 5 of R01AI110964 required EcoHealth to immediately notify its NIAID Program Officer and Grants Management Specialist if any experiments proposed in the award resulted in a virus with enhanced growth by more than one log compared to wild-type strains. The Notice of Award also stated that research involving the resulting virus(es) may require review under the HHS P3CO Framework.

According to NIH's evaluation of EcoHealth's progress report for Year 5 of the grant, NIH believed there was evidence that the research conducted by EcoHealth's subrecipient WIV during Year 5 resulted in enhanced growth by more than one log, thus triggering the special term and condition to immediately notify NIAID and potentially requiring the research to undergo review under the HHS P3CO Framework. NIH required immediate notification of this type of unexpected research result, because a one-log increase in growth has been used as a criteria for initiating a secondary review to determine whether the research aims should be evaluated or new biosafety measures should be enacted.

With respect to the issue of the special term and condition to provide "immediate notification" to NIAID, EcoHealth asserted that the experiment reported in the Year 5 progress report included results from a followup analysis of the same experiment conducted in Year 4 of the award and reported in the Year 4 progress report. However, based on NIH's Office of Extramural Research review of the progress reports for Year 4 and Year 5, NIH explained that it cannot determine whether Year 4's progress report included results from the same experiment.[17] EcoHealth believes it was in compliance with the requirement to immediately notify NIAID of the research results because EcoHealth reported the results in the Year 4 progress report. However, NIH does not believe reporting research in a progress report constitutes immediate notification. We agree with NIH's assessment that reporting research in a progress report does not constitute immediate notification; however, we did not find evidence that NIH clearly defined requirements related to the process and timeline EcoHealth should follow to provide immediate notification.

NIH Did Not Ensure EcoHealth Reported Required Subaward Data for Award R01AI110964

NIH's monitoring did not discover EcoHealth's noncompliance with requirements to report subawards for more than 5 years, which demonstrates that NIH's policies and procedures were not always effective. FFATA as amended requires most recipients of Federal funds awarded on or after October 1, 2010, to report on subawards and subcontracts equal to or greater than $25,000. Recipients use the FFATA Subawarding Reporting System (FSRS) to report their

---

[17] While NIH was not able to substantiate whether the Year 4 and Year 5 experiments were the same, NIH informed us that it does not believe that either experiment described is associated with severe acute respiratory syndrome coronavirus 2 (SARS-CoV-2) or the COVID-19 pandemic.

subawards. Prior to July 2020, EcoHealth had not complied with the subaward reporting requirement for at least 5 years. Not reporting required subaward information limits NIH and the general public's visibility into, and transparency of, how these grant funds were used. While EcoHealth was not in compliance with the disclosure requirements, it was not evident that NIH was aware of this failure until July 2020, when NIH required EcoHealth to comply with the disclosure requirements as one of the conditions of its grant suspension. Given that EcoHealth's first subaward covered the period June 1, 2014, through May 31, 2015, we believe NIH's monitoring of EcoHealth's grants should have revealed EcoHealth's failure to comply with the subaward disclosure requirement as early as 2016 during the renewal process for Year 3 of the award.

As part of its monitoring, NIH has access to recipient audit reports and financial statements. Based on our review of audit reports, we noted that EcoHealth's Schedule of Expenditures of Federal Awards (SEFA) included in its financial statements for the years ended June 30, 2016, June 30, 2017, June 30, 2018, and June 30, 2019, did not include the proper amounts of subaward funding for NIAID's Federal programs.[18] We would reasonably expect NIH's monitoring activities to detect this repeated reporting omission and then for NIH to advise EcoHealth to modify that section of its financial statements.

NIH Did Not Follow All Required Procedures To Terminate One of Its Grant Awards

Although NIH found EcoHealth to have several instances of noncompliance with award requirements, NIH did not follow Federal regulations and departmental policy to appropriately terminate one of EcoHealth's awards.

As part of NIH's monitoring of the R01AI110964 award to EcoHealth, NIH sent a letter to EcoHealth on April 19, 2020, requiring EcoHealth to cease providing any funds to its subrecipient WIV, citing concerns that WIV may have been involved with the release of the coronavirus responsible for COVID-19. On April 21, 2020, EcoHealth responded that it would comply with this request. Three days later, on April 24, 2020, NIH sent a letter informing EcoHealth that it was terminating the grant "for convenience," stating NIH did not believe the current project outcomes aligned with program goals and agency priorities.

We found several deficiencies with the notice NIH provided to EcoHealth terminating the award:

- NIH stated that it did not believe the current project outcomes aligned with program goals and agency priorities. Accordingly, the termination notice cited "for convenience" as the cause for termination; however, that is not a valid termination cause pursuant to

---

[18] As part of a grant recipient's financial statements, a recipient of a Federal grant award must prepare a SEFA that covers the period of the financial statements to disclose the total amount of a Federal award spent, subawards received, and amounts passed through to subrecipients.

45 CFR § 75.372.[19]

- The termination notice did not include a statement of EcoHealth's appeal rights as required by Federal regulations and NIH GPS.[20]

- There was no NIH official named on the termination notice to whom EcoHealth should submit an appeal, as required by NIH GPS.[21]

- The termination notice did not provide any sort of opportunity for EcoHealth to provide information and documentation challenging the termination action, as required by Federal regulations.[22]

On May 22, 2020, EcoHealth submitted a formal appeal to NIH, challenging the termination action. In absence of a specific person at NIH named on the termination notice to send an appeal to, EcoHealth addressed its appeal to the NIH Deputy Director for Extramural Research who signed the termination letter.

On July 8, 2020, NIH wrote to EcoHealth informing EcoHealth that NIH had withdrawn its termination of grant R01AI110964 and reinstated the grant. The letter went on to cite that NIH had received reports that WIV, one of EcoHealth's subrecipients, had been conducting research at WIV's facilities in China that posed serious biosafety concerns and, as a result, created health and welfare threats to the public in China and other countries. In this letter, NIH proceeded to suspend all activities related to R01AI110964 until concerns listed in the letter were addressed to NIH's satisfaction.[23] The notice cited that the suspension was taken in accord with 45 CFR § 75.371 and that the action was not appealable; however, EcoHealth could provide information and documentation demonstrating that WIV and EcoHealth had satisfied certain requirements.

GPAM (Part H, Chapter 4, Par. 21) states that the notice of post-award suspension of award activities must clearly indicate which corrective actions must occur during the enforcement action and an HHS operating division's intent to terminate the award if the recipient does not meet the conditions of the enforcement action.

---

[19] Appendix F contains Federal requirements associated with terminating and suspending grant awards.

[20] 45 CFR § 75.374(a) and NIH GPS, Section 8.7.

[21] NIH GPS, section 8.7.

[22] 45 CFR § 75.374(a).

[23] EcoHealth was to address certain items related to lab safety and oversight of WIV. During the period of suspension, EcoHealth was not to allow any research to be conducted under the suspended award, nor spend any grant funds associated with the suspended award.

NIH and EcoHealth had ongoing communications spanning a more than 2-year period addressing items related to the grant suspension. Most recently, on August 19, 2022, NIH sent a letter notifying EcoHealth of actions: (1) to terminate the subaward from EcoHealth to WIV; (2) to explore renegotiating the remainder of the award without involvement from WIV, and without a significant scientific departure from the original peer-reviewed project; and (3) if the remaining award could be renegotiated, to issue a revised award subject to specific award conditions. NIH noted that a partial termination is appealable. Because of these actions, we make no recommendations to NIH related to its initial termination of the R01AI110964 award to EcoHealth.

ECOHEALTH HAD POLICIES AND PROCEDURES TO MANAGE GRANT AWARDS AND MITIGATE POTENTIAL RISK BEFORE SUBAWARDING GRANT FUNDS

EcoHealth had policies and procedures to manage grant awards and mitigate potential risk before subawarding grant funds as we describe below. EcoHealth is responsible for the oversight of the operations of Federal award-supported activities and must monitor subrecipient activities under Federal awards to assure compliance with applicable Federal requirements and performance expectations are being achieved (45 CFR § 75.342(a)). In addition, in its role as a pass-through entity, EcoHealth must evaluate each subrecipient's risk of noncompliance with Federal statutes, regulations, and the terms and conditions of the subaward to determine the appropriate subrecipient monitoring.[24]

This risk assessment may consider factors such as:

- the subrecipient's prior experience with the same or similar subawards,

- the results of previous audits,

- whether the subrecipient has new personnel or new or substantially changed systems, and

- the extent and results of HHS awarding agency monitoring (e.g., whether the subrecipient also receives Federal awards directly from an HHS grant-awarding agency).

In February 2017, EcoHealth established a policy documenting its responsibility for monitoring the programmatic and financial activities of its subrecipients to ensure proper stewardship of sponsor funds to comply with the requirements of 45 CFR part 75. Among other things, the policy requires EcoHealth to monitor programmatic progress and the ability of the subrecipient to meet the objectives of the subaward, to complete risk assessments on new subrecipient organizations, and to conduct annual assessments on active subrecipient organizations. EcoHealth uses a risk-based approach to subrecipient monitoring, focusing on those

---

[24] 45 CFR § 75.352(b).

subrecipients deemed at greatest risk for noncompliance. See Table 2 for criteria EcoHealth used for assigning a level of risk.

Table 2: Factors for Assigning Level of Risk

- foreign versus domestic[25]
- maturity of organization
- subrecipient's prior experience with similar subawards or awarding agency
- adequacy of facilities[26]
- percentage of award passed through to subrecipient
- subrecipient familiarity with award mechanism
- audit results
- accounting/procurement systems
- scope of work and project deliverables
- familiarity of EcoHealth and subrecipient principal investigators
- rate of subrecipient spending on award
- subrecipient organization type

EcoHealth's risk analysis process included:

- checking the General Services Administration (GSA) System for Award Management (SAM) website to determine whether the subrecipient was suspended or debarred,

- verifying that the subrecipient had a compliant conflict of interest policy if required by the awarding agency, and

- verifying that the subrecipient maintained an adequate financial management system to account for award funds.

Based on our review of documentation that EcoHealth provided OIG, we found that EcoHealth officials met with WIV staff in person on at least 20 occasions between June 2014 and December 2019 and traveled to Wuhan, China, to meet with individuals from WIV at least annually during that time to discuss the research conducted under its subaward.[27] EcoHealth staff told OIG that they engaged in frequent phone calls and email exchanges with WIV staff throughout the grant period until the time the grant was terminated in April 2020.

Furthermore, since EcoHealth implemented its subrecipient monitoring policy in February 2017, we found that EcoHealth conducted risk assessments for each of its subrecipients. EcoHealth

---

[25] According to EcoHealth's risk checklist, foreign organizations are rated with "medium" or "high" risk, depending on the stability of the country's government and financial system.

[26] According to EcoHealth's risk checklist, this refers to whether the facilities are adequate and well-established; adequate and new; or inadequate.

[27] The documentation indicated that some meetings were at WIV.

also completed monitoring checklists for those subrecipients and conducted desk audits for selected subrecipients. Due to the COVID-19 pandemic, EcoHealth told OIG it had not conducted any in-person site visits at any of its subrecipients' facilities from January 2020 through the end of audit fieldwork in August 2022.

ECOHEALTH DID NOT ENSURE SUBAWARDS WERE COMPLIANT WITH FEDERAL REQUIREMENTS

Subaward Agreements Did Not Contain All Required Information

Contrary to Federal regulations, none of the subaward agreements contained all of the required information. Pursuant to 45 CFR § 75.352(a), each pass-through entity such as EcoHealth must ensure that each subaward is clearly identified as a subaward and must include specific information on the subrecipient agreement.[28]

Of the 11 subrecipient agreements we reviewed that EcoHealth used to subaward funding, all 11 agreements lacked at least 1 of these required elements.[29] This occurred because EcoHealth's policies and procedures did not ensure that the required data elements were included on each subaward. EcoHealth's noncompliance with these requirements limited the transparency of key Federal funding information to the subrecipients, such as the total amount of a Federal award committed to a subrecipient and the Federal award identification number. See Appendix H for details about subrecipient agreements lacking required data elements.

Inaccurate Subrecipient and Consultant Agreements

Some of the subrecipient and consultant agreements we reviewed were not written according to Federal regulations, which require non-Federal entities to maintain a financial management system that provides for the following:

- accurate, current, and complete disclosure of the financial results of each Federal award or program; and

- records that adequately identify sources and applications of funds for federally funded activities (45 CFR § 75.302(b)).

During our review of subrecipient and consultant agreements, we identified six agreements that contained inaccurate references to funding sources in EcoHealth's financial management system. In some cases, these incorrect references were in the form of unique grant identifiers in the accounting system; in other cases, written text in the agreement described a different funding source. According to EcoHealth, these errors occurred during copying and pasting of

---

[28] Appendix G contains a list of requirements associated with subrecipient agreements and monitoring.

[29] We also reviewed an additional subrecipient agreement, but it was not subject to these requirements because the agreement was signed prior to implementation of the requirements at 45 CFR § 75.352(a).

information from old agreements to new agreements. While we did not find evidence that the wrong funding source was used to pay subrecipients or consultants, it is possible that not all of EcoHealth's subrecipients or consultants were fully informed about the Federal funding source associated with their funding.

ECOHEALTH DID NOT ENSURE COMPLIANCE WITH REPORTING AND SUBRECIPIENT MONITORING REQUIREMENTS

The Progress Report Was Not Submitted in a Timely Manner for Year 5 of a Grant Award

As we described earlier in this report, EcoHealth submitted its Year 5 progress report late and the report involved research that NIH believed resulted in a virus with enhanced growth. EcoHealth's Notice of Award for Year 5 of R01AI110964 was issued on June 18, 2018. It had a budget period of June 1, 2018, to May 31, 2019. The Notice of Award required a final progress report be submitted within 120 days of the budget period's end date. Thus, EcoHealth should have submitted its progress report for Year 5 by the end of September 2019. We found evidence in the online system used to submit progress reports that EcoHealth initiated the progress report in July 2019; however, not until after NIH requested the progress report in July 2021 did EcoHealth submit the progress report on August 3, 2021, nearly 2 years late.

EcoHealth claimed that it had difficulty accessing the system used to submit progress reports, but we could not find evidence to support that claim. While we found that EcoHealth contacted NIH in late July 2019 in reference to the progress report, we did not find evidence that EcoHealth notified NIH about difficulty accessing the system used to submit progress reports. Furthermore, we found no evidence that NIH requested the progress report until July 2021. Due to late submission of the Year 5 progress report, EcoHealth was not in compliance with the report submission deadlines, which contributed to NIH not being made aware of the research results and not having information needed to understand the nature of research conducted in a timely manner.

EcoHealth Was Unable To Obtain Scientific Documentation From a Subrecipient

EcoHealth has been unable to provide NIH with certain scientific documentation in response to an NIH request. Federal regulations (45 CFR § 75.364(a)) require non-Federal entities to grant access to any documents, papers, or other records of the non-Federal entity that are pertinent to the Federal award to the HHS awarding agency, the Inspector General, or the pass-through entity. EcoHealth's subaward agreements state that EcoHealth may examine, audit, or have audited the records of the subrecipient as they relate to activities supported by the agreement.

On November 5, 2021, NIH requested that EcoHealth provide certain scientific documentation from WIV substantiating research covering EcoHealth's Year 4 (project period June 1, 2017, to May 31, 2018) and Year 5 (project period June 1, 2018, to May 31, 2019) progress reports to gain insights into the nature of the experiments that were performed.[30] In turn, EcoHealth requested the information from WIV. However, based on records reviewed, we did not see evidence that EcoHealth obtained the scientific documentation. EcoHealth officials confirmed to us that WIV had not been responsive to its request to provide the scientific documentation and indicated it was unlikely to receive the requested information. As a result, EcoHealth has been unable to comply with NIH's request on this matter. In a discussion of this specific matter with NIH's Deputy Director for Extramural Research, NIH acknowledged to OIG that WIV may never provide EcoHealth with the requested documentation. Although EcoHealth's subaward agreements had language permitting it to access the records of its subrecipients and also had policies and procedures to assess and monitor its subrecipients, EcoHealth has been limited in its ability to require WIV to take specific action or provide specific information. This has been due in part to the lack of cooperation by WIV, as reported by EcoHealth and NIH.

The approach in the governmentwide regulations that NIH follows related to oversight and monitoring of foreign subrecipients also contributed to this finding. These regulations are designed to have a prime grant recipient monitor the activities of a subrecipient, rather than requiring the grant-awarding agency—in this case, NIH—to conduct active monitoring of subrecipients. NIH expects its prime grant recipients to be accountable for performance of the research project, and it also expects prime grant recipients to address and report certain problems with its subrecipients to NIH—sometimes immediately. For foreign subrecipients, the effectiveness of the prime recipient's monitoring relies on the level of cooperation between the recipient and the subrecipient. In certain countries in which the research is performed, there may be a risk that larger political or governmental issues may impede cooperation and prime recipients will have limited ability to effectively monitor their foreign subrecipients.

As previously stated in this report, OIG has identified NIH's oversight of grants to foreign applicants as a potential risk to the Department in meeting program goals and the appropriate use of Federal funds. Additionally, prior OIG work has found foreign recipients at risk of noncompliance with grant requirements and maintaining documentation that is needed to effectively oversee and manage Federal grant awards.[31]

EcoHealth Did Not Comply With Certain Requirements Associated With Reporting Subaward Funding

Contrary to Federal regulations, EcoHealth did not properly report subawards in its SEFA or report them on the FSRS website. Regulations at 45 CFR § 75.510(b) require auditees to prepare a SEFA for the period covered by the auditee's financial statements. The SEFA must

---

[30] The scientific documentation requested consisted of complete and dated copies of the original laboratory notebook entries and original electronic files that led to the Year 4 and Year 5 progress reports.

[31] *Although CDC Implemented Corrective Actions To Improve Oversight of the President's Emergency Plan for AIDS Relief Recipients, Some Internal Control Weaknesses Remained*, A-04-18-01010, December 2020, available at https://oig.hhs.gov/oas/reports/region4/41801010.asp.

include the total Federal awards expended. Regulations at 45 CFR §§ 75.510(b)(2-4) require the recipient to list the name of each pass-through entity for which it received Federal subawarded funding and require the auditee to include the total amount provided to subrecipients from each Federal program.

The SEFA in EcoHealth's financial statements for the years ended June 30, 2016, June 30, 2017, June 30, 2018, and June 30, 2019, did not include the proper amount of subawarded funding for NIAID's Federal programs. EcoHealth stated that its independent accountants advised EcoHealth not to include that information; however, this advice was contrary to Federal reporting requirements. In addition, EcoHealth's failure to report the subaward funding limited NIH's access to accurate information in the audit report's SEFA to use in NIH's monitoring process.

FFATA requires most recipients of Federal funds awarded on or after October 1, 2010, to report on subawards and subcontracts equal to or greater than $25,000. Recipients use FSRS to report their subawards. Prior to July 2020, EcoHealth had not complied with the reporting requirement to report its subawards. Until NIH informed EcoHealth in July 2020 that it was not in compliance with these reporting requirements for its subawards, EcoHealth did not report any of its subawards on the FSRS website according to Federal requirements. During the audit, we noted EcoHealth did not have sufficient policies and procedures to address these reporting requirements.

ECOHEALTH DID NOT ALWAYS USE ITS GRANT FUNDS ACCORDING TO FEDERAL REQUIREMENTS

We determined that EcoHealth claimed $89,171 in costs that did not meet Federal requirements. These costs included salaries exceeding the NIH salary cap, employee bonuses, travel costs, tuition costs, indirect costs claimed by a subrecipient, other costs, and associated fringe and indirect costs. See Table 3 for a summary of unallowable costs by cost category.

Table 3: Summary of Unallowable Costs by Cost Category

Cost Category (Associated Grant Numbers)	Unallowable Direct Cost	Unallowable Fringe Benefit and Indirect Cost	Total Unallowable Cost
Salaries and Bonuses (All Grant Numbers)	$26,604*	$17,836	$44,440
Tuition (R01AI110964)	13,951	4,641	18,592
Indirect Costs Claimed by Subrecipient (R01AI110964)	13,037	0	13,037
Travel (R01AI110964)	5,752	1,876	7,628
Other (R01AI110964 and U01AI151797)	4,571	903	5,474
Unallowable Cost Totals	**$63,915**	**$25,256**	**$89,171**

* This amount includes $10,627 and $15,977 in unallowable salary and bonus costs, respectively.

Federal regulations at 45 CFR § 75.403 require that costs:

- be necessary and reasonable for the performance of the Federal award and be allocable under these principles,

- conform to any limitations or exclusions set forth in these principles or in the Federal award,

- be consistent with policies and procedures that apply uniformly to both federally financed activities and other activities of the non-Federal entity, and

- be adequately documented.

Salary Costs Exceeded the NIH Salary Cap

We determined that $10,627 in sampled salary costs for selected EcoHealth employees were claimed in excess of the NIH salary cap. NIH funds shall not be used to pay the salary of an individual through a grant or other extramural mechanism at a rate in excess of that prescribed. Applications and proposals with categorical, direct-cost budgets reflecting direct salaries of individuals in excess of the rate prescribed are to be adjusted according to the legislative salary limitation (NIH GPS, section 4.2.10). For our audit period, NIH's salary cap ranged from $181,500 to $199,300 for recipient employees fully allocated to NIH grant awards. For recipient employees whose salaries are partially funded by NIH grant awards, the salary cap is adjusted proportionally to the amount of effort charged to the NIH award.

While EcoHealth indicated that it was aware of the NIH salary cap and properly accounted for it, we determined that EcoHealth did not consider the percent of effort assigned to the grant, resulting in amounts paid with NIH grant funds in excess of the salary cap.

EcoHealth Provided Employee Bonuses Without an Established Plan and Claimed Unallowable Indirect and Fringe Benefits

We identified $15,977 in employee bonuses that were improperly paid with NIH grant funds to seven EcoHealth employees. The bonuses paid were not in accordance with NIH GPS requirements. The NIH GPS states that "Incentive compensation to employees based on cost reduction, or efficient performance, suggestion awards, safety awards, etc., is allowable to the extent that the overall compensation is determined to be reasonable and such costs are paid or accrued pursuant to an agreement entered into in good faith between the non-Federal entity and the employees before the services were rendered, or pursuant to an established plan followed by the non-Federal entity so consistently as to imply, in effect, an agreement to make such payment." (NIH GPS, section 7.9.1)

EcoHealth's policy on Performance Management states that positive performance evaluations do not guarantee increases in salary, bonus payments, or any other type of discretionary compensation. Promotions, salary increases, and discretionary payments of any kind are solely under the discretion of management and depend upon many factors in addition to individual performance (EcoHealth Employee Handbook, chapter 19).

We determined that all $15,977 in bonuses we reviewed were unallowable because there was no agreement entered into between EcoHealth and the employees before the services were rendered. Nor do we believe the language in EcoHealth's Employee Handbook meets the requirements listed in NIH GPS as it relates to having an established plan to pay bonuses. The language in EcoHealth's Employee Handbook is too vague to be an agreement to make a bonus payment or an established plan that is followed so consistently as to imply an agreement to make a bonus payment. EcoHealth believed that charging employee bonuses to NIH grants was allowable.

In addition to the unallowable salary costs in excess of NIH's salary cap and unallowable bonus costs, we determined that associated indirect and fringe benefit costs that EcoHealth paid with NIH grant funds of $17,836 were also unallowable.

Tuition Costs Did Not Meet Federal Requirements

We determined that EcoHealth claimed unallowable Ph.D. education tuition costs for an EcoHealth employee enrolled at Kingston University, located in London, England. The claims were made to the R01AI110964 research grant in the amounts of $4,603 and $9,348 for the

2018–19 and 2019–20 academic years, respectively. Regulations at 45 CFR § 75.472 specifically allow for the cost of training and education provided for employee development. However, section 7.9.1 of NIH GPS states that trainee costs are allowable only under predoctoral and postdoctoral training grants.

EcoHealth explained that it believed paying tuition costs with NIH grant funds was allowable. According to the NIH GPS, that is true only in limited cases involving a specific type of NIH grant award, and EcoHealth's grant was not of this limited type. Accordingly, we identified a total of $13,951 in unallowable tuition costs, along with $4,641 in associated indirect costs.

Indirect Costs Were Claimed in Excess of Allowable Rates for Foreign Subawards

We determined that EcoHealth claimed $13,037 in unallowable indirect costs associated with subawards at WIV. Facilities and administrative costs under grants to foreign and international organizations will be funded at a fixed rate of 8 percent of modified total direct costs, exclusive of tuition and related fees, direct expenditures for equipment, and subawards in excess of $25,000. These funds are paid to support the costs of compliance with Federal requirements (NIH GPS, section 7.4).

For four sampled claims, we determined that WIV claimed indirect costs at a rate of 11 percent, or 3 percent greater than the allowable rate of 8 percent.

Travel Costs Did Not Meet Federal Requirements

We determined that $5,752 in travel costs paid with NIH grant funds were unallowable for the reasons listed below. Travel costs are allowable as a direct cost when providing a direct benefit to the grant-funded project. Consistent with the organization's established travel policy, these costs for employees working on a grant-supported project may include associated per diem or subsistence allowances and other travel-related expenses. If a recipient organization has no established travel policy, Federal Travel Regulations issued by GSA will be used to determine the amount that may be charged for travel costs. Those regulations include maximum per diem and subsistence rates. Alcohol is generally an unallowable expense (NIH GPS, section 7.9.1).

We determined that a payment totaling $3,285 for the transportation and accommodation costs of an EcoHealth employee attending a conference in October 2016 was unallowable. The employee was traveling under a non-NIH grant. Travel costs are required to provide direct benefit to the grant-funded project.[32] A coding mistake resulted in the charge to the NIH-funded grant, and EcoHealth concurred with our determination.

We determined that a payment totaling $2,128 for a meeting room and meal costs at a hotel on February 3, 2016, was unallowable. The support provided for the claim was an attestation of

---

[32] GPS Section 7.9.1.

expenses. Travel costs are required to be supported by source documentation and be adequately documented.[33] EcoHealth noted that the original receipt had been lost. EcoHealth officials documented the costs to the best of their knowledge. The attestation is not sufficient to support the claiming of costs to the grant.

We identified a claim for a one-night hotel stay on April 14, 2015, totaling $601, which was above the allowable per diem amount of $268. The hotel costs above the per diem rate totaled $334 and were unallowable. Also included on this invoice was a claim for an alcoholic beverage totaling $5 that was unallowable, for a total of $339 in unallowable costs. Travel costs must be made according to established per diem rates and for allowable purposes.[34]

According to the indirect rates EcoHealth used at the time each of these payments were made, we computed an additional $1,876 in unallowable indirect costs associated with the unallowable travel payments.

Other Costs Did Not Meet Federal Requirements

Visa Costs

We identified an invoice for which EcoHealth claimed reimbursement for expedited processing fees for an H-1B visa totaling $2,500. Visa costs are generally allowable as part of recruiting costs on an NIH grant as long as they are incurred to recruit a new employee and result in the institution having an employee/employer relationship with the individual.[35] Expedited processing fees are generally unallowable unless and until they become part of standard processing fees (NIH GPS, section 7.9.1).

EcoHealth believed that the expedited processing was required due to a backlog in visa processing. We express no opinion as to the necessity of expedited processing; however, the $2,500 portion of the invoice covering expedited processing charged to NIH grants, along with the $896 in associated indirect costs, are not allowable.

Invoice-Related Overpayments

EcoHealth claimed $2,078 in invoice-related overpayments. In general, NIH grant awards provide for reimbursement of actual, allowable costs incurred and are subject to Federal cost principles. A cost may be considered reasonable if the nature of the goods or services acquired or applied and the associated dollar amount reflect the action that a prudent person would have taken under the circumstances prevailing when the decision to incur the cost was made.

---

[33] 45 CFR § 75.302(b)(3) and 45 CFR § 75.403(g).

[34] GPS Section 7.9.1.

[35] Temporary worker visas are for persons who want to enter the United States for employment lasting a fixed period of time, and are not considered permanent or indefinite.

A cost is allocable to a cost objective—that is, a specific grant, function, department, or other component—if the goods or services involved are chargeable or assignable to that cost objective according to the relative benefits received or other equitable relationship (NIH GPS, section 7.2).

EcoHealth claimed $2,052 in unallowable costs associated with a subaward to WIV. The subrecipient submitted an invoice that contained a duplicate charge for in vitro studies, and the amount was added twice to arrive at the total invoiced amount. Separately, a consultant requested a payment of $15,000, but the detailed invoice only totaled $14,981, or $19 less than the actual payment. EcoHealth paid the consultant the full $15,000, resulting in a $19 overpayment from the detailed invoice, and $7 in associated indirect costs.

POTENTIAL UNREIMBURSED COSTS FOR A GRANT AWARD

As of May 2022, EcoHealth provided us with documentation to demonstrate that it had unreimbursed costs of approximately $74,500. EcoHealth claims that these costs were the result of adjustments to fringe benefits and indirect cost rates that occurred after the initial claims were submitted. We did not independently verify the accuracy of this computation; however, NIH should perform further analysis to determine whether EcoHealth had any incurred, unreimbursed costs for grant R01AI110964. The notices of termination and suspension to EcoHealth did not indicate which costs NIH would reimburse if the enforcement action were lifted and the award resumed.

NIH notified EcoHealth on April 24, 2020, that it elected to terminate the project Understanding the Risk of Bat Coronavirus Emergence, funded under grant R01AI110964, for convenience. Later, on July 8, 2020, NIH notified EcoHealth that it withdrew its termination of grant R01AI110964 and reinstated the grant. However, in the same letter NIH suspended all activities related to R01AI110964 until these concerns have been addressed to NIH's satisfaction, citing 45 CFR § 75.371, Remedies for Noncompliance, and several GPS citations.

GPAM (Part H, Chapter 4, Par. 21) requires that the notice of post-award suspension of award activities must clearly indicate which costs the HHS operating division will reimburse if the enforcement action is ultimately lifted and the award resumed. Additionally, NIH GPS (section 7.9.1) provides that NIH will allow full credit to a recipient for the Federal share of otherwise allowable costs if the obligations are properly incurred by the recipient before suspension or termination—and not in anticipation of suspension or termination—and, in the case of termination, are not cancellable. The Grants Management Officer may authorize other costs in, or subsequent to, the notice of termination or suspension.

CONCLUSION

Despite identifying potential risks associated with research being performed under the EcoHealth awards, NIH did not effectively monitor or take timely action to address EcoHealth's compliance with some research requirements. After the Federal governmentwide pause on gain-of-function research was lifted, HHS and NIH implemented specific procedures to assess and monitor research reasonably anticipated to create, transfer, or use an ePPP. Given the inherent risks of this type of work, NIAID had a policy to err on the side of inclusion when considering whether to refer potential ePPP research to the NIAID DURC/P3CO Committee under the P3CO process. NIH determined that research under EcoHealth awards did not involve ePPP research, and as such, did not refer the proposed research to the HHS P3CO Committee for additional review. Nevertheless, NIH added a special term and condition in EcoHealth's awards requiring immediate notification if the research resulted in certain specified benchmarks involving log growth increases.

NIH provided limited guidance on how EcoHealth should comply with this specific requirement. EcoHealth never provided separate notice under that special term and condition because EcoHealth believed annual progress reports would constitute immediate notification. In addition, EcoHealth did not in a timely manner submit an annual progress report, nor did NIH in a timely manner follow up on the late report until nearly 2 years after its due date. Although NIH concluded the progress report identified virus growth that met certain benchmarks, EcoHealth's inability to obtain scientific documentation from WIV limited NIH's ability to assess EcoHealth's position that it had notified NIH/NIAID of meeting certain benchmarks in the Year 4 progress report and possibly conclude whether the research involved ePPP. As a result, NIH missed opportunities to more effectively monitor EcoHealth's research. With improved oversight, NIH may have been able to take more timely corrective actions to mitigate the inherent risks associated with this type of research.

Lapses in complying with NIH's monitoring procedures limited NIH and EcoHealth's ability to effectively monitor Federal grant awards and subawards to understand the nature of the research conducted, identify potential problem areas, and take necessary corrective action. Furthermore, these lapses limited NIH and EcoHealth's ability to determine how these grant funds were used, and mitigate the risk of noncompliance with Federal requirements and internal policies and procedures.

Our oversight work has continually demonstrated that grant-awarding agencies' oversight of subrecipients, whether domestic or foreign, is challenging. This is partly due to governmentwide regulations that NIH follows that are designed to have a prime grant recipient monitor the activities of a subrecipient, rather than requiring the grant-awarding agency—in this case NIH—to conduct active monitoring of subrecipients. For foreign subrecipients, the effectiveness of the prime recipient's monitoring may depend on the level of cooperation between the recipient and the subrecipient. In certain countries in which research is performed, there may be a risk that larger political or governmental issues may impede cooperation and prime recipients will have limited ability to effectively monitor their foreign subrecipients. Although documentation indicates that WIV cooperated with EcoHealth's monitoring for several years, WIV's lack of cooperation with the international community following the COVID-19 outbreak—consistent with the response from China—limited EcoHealth's ability to monitor its subrecipient, and greater transparency is needed about information from WIV.[36] While the larger risks associated with political or governmental challenges may be hard to fully address under the grant process, NIH should assess how it can best mitigate these issues and ensure that it can oversee the use of NIH funds by foreign recipients and subrecipients.

We believe NIH has begun to take action to address some issues found in our audit. However, additional work is needed to ensure that NIH is able to fulfill its mission to enhance health, reduce illness and disability, and ensure grant funds are used for their intended purpose.

RECOMMENDATIONS

We recommend that the National Institutes of Health:[37]

1. ensure that EcoHealth accurately and in a timely manner reports award and subaward information, including in:

    a. recipient progress reports;

    b. the Federal Funding Accountability and Transparency Act of 2006, Subawarding Reporting System; and

    c. recipient-audited financial statements;

2. implement enhanced monitoring, documentation, and reporting requirements for recipients with foreign subrecipients;

3. define the process and timeline for what NIH considers "immediate notification" as it relates to specific award conditions intended to report unexpected research outcomes;

4. ensure that administrative actions such as terminations are performed in compliance with Federal regulations and HHS policies and procedures, and appropriate notifications of appeal rights are provided;

5. work with EcoHealth to recover identified unallowable costs, along with salary costs in excess of the NIH salary cap and bonus costs that were not sampled;

6. work with EcoHealth to determine whether EcoHealth had any unreimbursed costs at the time award R01AI110964 was terminated;

---

[36] As reported by the National Intelligence Council, China has likely impeded investigations related to the origins of COVID-19.

[37] The recommendations to NIH and EcoHealth are numbered to correspond with how each entity labeled the corresponding recommendation in its comments on the draft report.

7. assess whether NIAID staff are following the NIAID P3CO policy, including erring on the side of inclusion when determining whether proposed research should be referred to the NIAID DURC/P3CO Committee for research proposals that may involve ePPP;

8. based on information provided in this audit and any other information available to NIH, consider whether it is appropriate to refer WIV to HHS for debarment and exercise continued monitoring and enforcement activities as appropriate over the course of the grant awards and subawards; and

9. ensure for any future NIH grant awards that EcoHealth has addressed the deficiencies noted in the report.

We recommend that EcoHealth Alliance:

1. prepare subaward and consultant agreements that contain all required information and are accurate,

2. submit progress reports by the required due date,

3. comply with requirements to immediately notify NIH of conditions that materially impact the ability to meet award objectives,

4. ensure that it has the ability to access all records related to its research conducted at subrecipient locations,

5. properly identify subawards in financial statements, and

6. report subawards according to FFATA requirements.

We recommend EcoHealth Alliance refund to the Government $89,171 in unallowable costs consisting of:

1. salary costs claimed in excess of the NIH salary cap totaling $10,627,

2. bonus costs totaling $15,977,

3. indirect and fringe benefits associated with salary and bonus costs totaling $17,836,

4. Ph.D. education tuition costs totaling $13,951 and associated indirect costs of $4,641,

5. indirect costs totaling $13,037 claimed by a subrecipient,

6. travel costs totaling $5,752 and associated indirect costs of $1,876,

7. visa costs of $2,500 and associated indirect costs of $896,

8. subaward costs of $2,052, and

9. professional fees costs of $19 and associated indirect costs of $7.

NATIONAL INSTITUTES OF HEALTH AND ECOHEALTH COMMENTS AND OFFICE OF INSPECTOR GENERAL RESPONSE

In written comments, NIH stated that it concurred or generally concurred with our recommendations and provided actions taken or planned to address them. EcoHealth stated it concurred with our first recommendation but did not directly state whether it concurred or did not concur with the remaining recommendations. EcoHealth identified two substantive areas of disagreement with the reported findings: (1) the timeliness of EcoHealth's Year 5 progress report and (2) whether an experiment exhibited "enhanced growth."

After reviewing the comments, we maintain that all of our findings and recommendations are valid. Below, we separately describe NIH's and EcoHealth's comments and provide OIG responses, as applicable.

NIH COMMENTS FOR RECOMMENDATIONS 1 THROUGH 9

Regarding recommendations 1, 4, and 8, NIH concurred and provided additional support on actions implementing the OIG recommendations. On August 19, 2022, NIH notified EcoHealth of specific award conditions to address accurate and timely reports of award and subaward information. These conditions included onsite subrecipient facility inspections every 6 months, withdrawal of automatic no-cost extensions and carryover authorities, and a requirement to submit semiannual progress reports. Furthermore, NIH stated that it will ensure that administrative actions are performed in compliance with Federal regulations.

Regarding recommendations 3, 5, 6, and 9, NIH concurred and noted actions that it will perform within 90 days of the publication of the report that will address the recommendations. The procedures include revising NIH policies to include a definition for the process and timeline for immediate notification as it related to unexpected research outcomes, working with EcoHealth to recover any identified unallowable costs, and determining whether EcoHealth had unreimbursed costs at the time the R01AI110964 award was terminated. Furthermore, NIH stated it will work with EcoHealth to ensure that the deficiencies noted in this report are being satisfactorily addressed.

Regarding recommendation 2, NIH generally concurred and stated that it will evaluate best practices across the Government for overseeing awards issued to domestic recipients that, in turn, oversee foreign subrecipients. Regarding recommendation 7, NIH concurred and has established a working group to assess the current process for review and oversight of proposed research involving ePPPs.[38]

NIH also provided technical comments on our draft report, which we addressed as appropriate. NIH's comments, excluding technical comments, are included in their entirety as Appendix I.

OFFICE OF INSPECTOR GENERAL RESPONSE

We appreciate the cooperation NIH provided during the course of our audit and the proactive steps taken thus far to address our report findings and recommendations.

ECOHEALTH COMMENTS FOR RECOMMENDATIONS 1, 5, AND 6

Regarding recommendations 1, 5, and 6, EcoHealth noted that it had implemented procedures or taken actions to address the recommendations and related findings. EcoHealth stated that it has updated and revised its subaward and consultant agreements to contain required language and subaward identification, and has instituted measures to correct omissions on the agreements. EcoHealth further stated that it has instituted policies to ensure that it properly identifies subawards in its financial statements, and has provided all required FFATA reporting forms requested by NIH.

OFFICE OF INSPECTOR GENERAL RESPONSE

We appreciate the cooperation EcoHealth provided during the course of our audit and the proactive steps taken thus far to address our report findings and recommendations.

ECOHEALTH COMMENTS FOR RECOMMENDATION 2

Regarding recommendation 2, EcoHealth stated that it will continue to submit all required progress reports and indicated disagreement with the OIG finding that EcoHealth submitted its R01AI110964 Year 5 progress report late. EcoHealth stated that the Year 5 progress report was written and uploaded to the NIH online portal for submission by EcoHealth staff in July 2019, ahead of the September deadline. However, when EcoHealth staff attempted to submit the Year 5 report during late July 2019, the grant had been renewed for an additional 5 years, and the NIH system locked EcoHealth out from submitting the report. EcoHealth stated that NIH staff did not follow up with a request to EcoHealth for a Year 5 report, NIH did not answer EcoHealth's direct questions, and NIH did not return phone calls. EcoHealth noted the fact that because the new award was made, work was allowed to continue, and no requests for an official Year 5 report submission were made by NIH, which suggested to EcoHealth staff that they were in compliance with the submission requirement.

---

[38] NIH has established the working group of the National Science Advisory Board for Biosecurity, a Federal advisory committee that addresses issues related to biosecurity and dual-use research, at the request of the Government.

OFFICE OF INSPECTOR GENERAL RESPONSE

We acknowledge in our report that EcoHealth's Year 5 progress report was initiated on NIH's online portal in July 2019; however, we have no evidence that the progress report was fully uploaded to the online portal at that time. Furthermore, we have no evidence that there was any correspondence between EcoHealth and NIH describing technical difficulties with uploading the progress report on time. Ultimately, the progress report was not submitted until August 2021.

ECOHEALTH COMMENTS FOR RECOMMENDATION 3

Regarding recommendation 3, EcoHealth stated it will continue to comply with requirements to notify NIH of conditions that materially impact its ability to meet award objectives, and indicated disagreement with the OIG finding that it did not immediately notify NIH of conditions that materially impact its ability to meet award objectives. On the issue of timely reporting results to NIH, EcoHealth stated that: (1) the amended annual Notice of Award document did not use the phrase "immediately notify" and (2) NIH failed to provide a timeframe for notification in either the letter indicating that these experiments were approved or in the NIH Notice of Award. EcoHealth further stated that it did, in fact, notify NIH in a timely manner about these results by reporting the results of the experiment in an earlier progress report. In addition, EcoHealth stated that OIG made an incorrect statement in the report.

Specifically, EcoHealth stated OIG was incorrect in stating that NIH believed there was evidence that the research conducted by EcoHealth's subrecipient WIV during Year 5 resulted in "enhanced growth," thus triggering the special term and condition to immediately notify NIAID and potentially requiring the research undergo review under the HHS P3CO Framework. EcoHealth stated that the contention that it failed to report enhanced growth that would have required additional P3CO review as gain-of-function research was based on a misinterpretation of what the experiment in question actually showed. Specifically, EcoHealth indicated that it had reported on the same experiment in its Year 4 report submitted on time in 2018, and at that time EcoHealth had emailed a copy of its submitted Year 4 report to NIH and requested a timeslot to discuss the Year 4 report, the planned Year 5 work, and a renewal proposal.

OFFICE OF INSPECTOR GENERAL RESPONSE

The Notice of Award dated June 18, 2018, associated with the Year 5 funding, requires EcoHealth to notify NIAID grants officials immediately if certain benchmarks are met involving log growth increases and was what we used to determine whether EcoHealth's actions aligned with terms and conditions of the award. Furthermore, as we indicate in this report, our audit did not assess scientific results for any of the experiments or make any determination regarding the accuracy of NIH's or EcoHealth's interpretations of the Years 4 and 5 research results. Our audit found that NIH's own evaluation of the Year 5 progress report concluded that the research was of a type that should have been reported immediately to NIH. In an associated recommendation to NIH, we recommended NIH define the process and timeline for what NIH considers "immediate notification." We agreed with NIH's assessment that reporting research in a progress report does not constitute immediate notification.

ECOHEALTH COMMENTS FOR RECOMMEDATION 4

Regarding recommendation 4, EcoHealth stated that, to the best of its ability, it will do all possible to ensure it can access and supply all records related to research conducted at subrecipient locations. However, it finds misleading the reported statement that it was unable to obtain scientific documentation from a subrecipient. EcoHealth notes a number of events that impacted its ability to access certain records, specifically that NIH instructed EcoHealth to cease the provision of funds to WIV 18 months before NIH requested EcoHealth obtain records from WIV, termination of the R01AI110964 grant, and significant geopolitical pressure and media coverage related to WIV, EcoHealth, and NIH-funded research.

OFFICE OF INSPECTOR GENERAL RESPONSE

OIG's report recognizes the impact that the COVID-19 outbreak had on EcoHealth's ability to receive cooperation from WIV. Furthermore, we recognize the general limitations associated with oversight of foreign subrecipients by prime recipients. However, EcoHealth is required by Federal regulations to ensure access to records from WIV. This record access requirement is important to ensure grantees are accountable for funds provided and that results of the research are available to NIH. The challenges EcoHealth experienced in getting records from WIV provides support for OIG's recommendation to NIH to enhance monitoring of foreign subrecipients so that NIH can take steps to mitigate the risks that non-cooperation by foreign Governments may pose to future awards and associated research.

ECOHEALTH COMMENTS FOR THE NINE MONETARY RECOMMENDATIONS

Regarding the nine monetary recommendations, EcoHealth stated that it reimbursed NIH for the total reported unallowable costs and provided NIH with details on the amounts of allowable but unreimbursed costs. However, EcoHealth disagreed with the OIG interpretation of Federal requirements for some items of cost and is seeking clarification from NIH. Specifically, EcoHealth stated that bonus costs are incentive payment allocations that may be deemed allowable under existing Federal guidelines, and that the bonuses and associated fringe benefit and indirect costs are allowable. EcoHealth disagreed with the questioning of Ph.D. education tuition costs, as the staff member is undergoing training in research methodology that is within the scope and type of research conducted through the NIH-funded project. EcoHealth disagreed with the questioned costs associated with one travel cost that was missing travel expense documentation but for which EcoHealth submitted corroborating documentation including price estimates, traveler information, and meeting agendas. EcoHealth disagreed with the questioned costs for visa costs and stated that the expense was justifiable given the need to rapidly engage an employee with a highly specialized skill set and background.

OFFICE OF INSPECTOR GENERAL RESPONSE

We maintain that all of our monetary recommendations are valid and in accordance with Federal regulations and the NIH Grants Policy Statement. Despite EcoHealth not fully agreeing with our interpretation of some of these requirements, EcoHealth stated that it did, in fact, repay the full amount of reported unallowable costs to NIH.[39] EcoHealth did not provide us with any new information or documentation that supported revising any reported unallowable costs. EcoHealth did request further clarification from NIH on certain costs, and we will review any guidance provided by NIH.

EcoHealth's comments are included in their entirety as Appendix J.

---

[39] As part of our audit recommendation followup process, we will request documentation that supports any repayment of funds to NIH for the unallowable costs we identified in this report.

APPENDIX A: AUDIT SCOPE AND METHODOLOGY

SCOPE

We obtained a list of all NIH grant and cooperative agreement awards to EcoHealth, and all subawards made by EcoHealth during the period FY 2014 through FY 2021. Our audit covered three NIH awards to EcoHealth totaling approximately $8.0 million, which included $1.8 million of EcoHealth's subawards to eight subrecipients. Appendix E includes a detailed list of EcoHealth's NIH awards and subawards.

We selected 150 transactions totaling $2,578,567 from EcoHealth's accounting system to determine whether the costs claimed were in compliance with Federal requirements. We used a nonstatistical methodology to select the transactions, which covered costs claimed under the three grants in our audit. We focused our selection on ensuring coverage of costs over our entire audit period, while including a variety of costs such as salaries, fringe benefits, subawards, professional fees, travel, supplies, telephone, publication, and indirect costs.

Of the 150 transactions we selected for review:

- 92 transactions were from grant number R01AI110964 totaling $1,525,012,

- 43 transactions were from grant number U01AI151797 totaling $751,949, and

- 15 transactions were from grant number U01AI153420 totaling $301,606.

We reviewed the transactions in accord with the cost principles in 45 CFR part 75 and with additional requirements located in the NIH GPS.

We determined that internal control was significant to our audit objectives. We assessed internal controls and compliance with laws and regulations necessary to satisfy the audit objectives, which included a review of NIH and EcoHealth's policies and procedures related to using, managing, and monitoring grant funds. However, because our review was limited to these aspects of internal control, it may not have disclosed all internal control deficiencies that may have existed at the time of this audit. Any internal control deficiencies we found are discussed in this report.

We conducted our fieldwork from June 2021 to August 2022, which included visiting EcoHealth's offices in New York City.

METHODOLOGY

To accomplish our first audit objective, we:

- interviewed NIH and NIAID officials familiar with the grant award and monitoring process;

- reviewed email communications and other correspondence between NIH and EcoHealth to gain insight on the types of interactions that occurred during the performance of the grant awards;

- reviewed Peer Review Summary Statements;

- reviewed required financial and programmatic reports;

- reviewed NIH oversight of EcoHealth's compliance with terms and conditions stated in the Notices of Award;

- reviewed NIH's oversight and reporting requirements associated with enhanced potential pandemic pathogens;

- as applicable, reviewed steps NIH took to ensure research was not anticipated to create, use, or transfer enhanced potential pandemic pathogens; and

- discussed the results of our audit with NIH.

To accomplish our second audit objective, we:

- interviewed EcoHealth officials familiar with the grant award and monitoring process,

- reviewed EcoHealth's policies and procedures,

- reviewed EcoHealth's subrecipient agreements,

- reviewed EcoHealth's subrecipient risk assessments,

- reviewed EcoHealth's subrecipient monitoring checklists,

- reviewed required financial and programmatic reports that EcoHealth submitted to NIH,

- selected and reviewed 150 transactions across the 3 NIH awards comprised of different types of transactions for allowability, and

- discussed the results of our audit with EcoHealth.

We conducted this performance audit in accordance with generally accepted government auditing standards. Those standards require that we plan and perform the audit to obtain sufficient, appropriate evidence to provide a reasonable basis for our findings and conclusions based on our audit objectives. We believe that the evidence obtained provides a reasonable basis for our findings and conclusions based on our audit objectives.

APPENDIX B: REQUIREMENTS ASSOCIATED WITH REVIEWING RESEARCH INVOLVING ENHANCED POTENTIAL PANDEMIC PATHOGENS

NIH describes potential pandemic pathogens as bacteria, viruses, and other microorganisms that are likely highly transmissible and capable of wide, uncontrollable spread in human populations as well as highly virulent, making them likely to cause significant morbidity and/or mortality in humans. On limited occasions, when NIH determines it is justified by compelling public health need and conducted in very high biosecurity laboratories, NIH has supported certain research that may be reasonably anticipated to create, transfer, or use potential pandemic pathogens resulting from the enhancement of a pathogen's transmissibility or virulence in humans. The Government and HHS define such research as ePPP research. NIH-supported ePPP research requires strict oversight and may only be conducted with appropriate biosafety and biosecurity measures.

The White House Office of Science and Technology Policy and HHS announced on October 17, 2014, that the Government was launching a deliberative process to assess the potential risks and benefits associated with a subset of life sciences research known as "gain-of-function" studies. During the period of deliberation, the Government instituted a pause on funding for any new studies that include certain gain-of-function experiments involving influenza, SARS, and MERS viruses. Specifically, the funding pause applied to gain-of-function research projects that may be reasonably anticipated to confer attributes to influenza, MERS, or SARS viruses such that the virus would have enhanced pathogenicity and/or transmissibility in mammals via the respiratory route. During this pause, the Government was not funding any new projects involving these experiments and encouraged those conducting this type of work—whether federally funded or not—to voluntarily pause their research while risks and benefits were reassessed. The funding pause did not apply to the characterization or testing of naturally occurring influenza, MERS, and SARS viruses unless there was a reasonable expectation that these tests would increase transmissibility and/or pathogenicity.

The HHS P3CO Framework was established in 2017. The HHS P3CO Framework describes measures responsive to and in accordance with the White House Office of Science and Technology Policy guidance to assess the potential risks and benefits associated with ePPPs. The Department's adoption of the HHS P3CO Framework satisfies the requirement for lifting the research funding pause on certain gain-of-function research. The HHS P3CO Framework is intended to guide HHS funding decisions on research that is reasonably anticipated to create, transfer, or use ePPPs.[40]

NIAID implemented the HHS P3CO Framework by developing a standard operating procedure *NIAID Extramural Potential Pandemic Pathogen Care and Oversight (P3CO)*. This procedure

---

[40] The U.S. Government Accountability Office report *HHS Could Improve Oversight of Research Involving Enhanced Potential Pandemic Pathogens*, GAO-23-105455, January 2023, available at https://www.gao.gov/products/gao-23-105455, found unclear policy and other policy gaps that may allow proposed research involving altered pathogens with pandemic potential to occur without appropriate oversight.

indicates that NIAID's P3CO risk assessment process begins with a review by program staff of all applications, proposals, supplements, and progress reports being considered for funding that involve research with a PPP. When NIAID program staff review proposed research involving a PPP, they shall err on the side of inclusion and refer proposed research that may be subject to the HHS P3CO Framework to the NIAID DURC/P3CO Committee to determine whether the research is subject to the HHS P3CO Framework review process. See Table 4 for roles and responsibilities of funding agencies and HHS.

Table 4: Summary of Funding Agency and Department Responsibilities Under the HHS P3CO Framework

Entity	Responsibilities
Funding Agency	<ul><li>Conduct standard scientific merit review</li><li>Refer proposed research that is reasonably anticipated to create, transfer, or use ePPPs to department-level review</li><li>Provide relevant information necessary to department-level review</li><li>Participate in department-level review process, as requested</li><li>Consider recommendations resulting from department-level review</li><li>Make funding decision, stipulating terms and conditions of award including additional risk mitigation measures, if appropriate</li><li>Report relevant information on funding decisions to HHS and the White House Office of Science and Technology Policy</li><li>Ensure implementation of and adherence to required risk mitigation procedures and other terms and/or conditions of award, if funded</li></ul>
HHS	<ul><li>Convene multidisciplinary group to review proposed research determined by funding agency as being reasonably anticipated to create, transfer, or use ePPPs</li><li>Critically evaluate proposed research including risk-benefit assessment and proposed risk mitigation plan</li><li>Consider eight criteria for guiding HHS funding decisions and additional relevant factors and information</li><li>Develop recommendations on acceptability for HHS funding, including suggestions for additional risk mitigation measures and/or terms and conditions of award, if funded</li></ul>

APPENDIX C: PEER REVIEW OF ECOHEALTH APPLICATIONS

NIH performed scientific peer reviews of the three EcoHealth grant applications covered under our audit scope prior to making the awards. The R01AI110964 and U01AI153420 reviews were conducted by the Clinical Research and Field Studies of Infectious Diseases Study Section, Infectious Diseases and Microbiology Integrated Review Group. The U01AI151797 review was performed by the NIAID Special Emphasis Panel Emerging Infectious Diseases Research Centers. The applications were scored at acceptable levels for further discussion and award approval. The results of a peer review are provided in a document known as a summary statement. A summary statement provides an overall summary of a review, critiques by reviewers, priority scores, budget recommendations, and administrative notes.

The peer review summary statement for the R01AI110964 application noted that the proposed studies were to determine factors that increase the risk of zoonotic CoV emergence in people by studying CoV diversity in a critical zoonotic reservoir (bats) at sites of high risk for emergence (wildlife markets) in an emerging disease hotspot (China). The statement provided that, given the SARS outbreak in 2002 and the emergence of MERS, the research is significant as it relates to advancing knowledge of the zoonotic potential of coronaviruses.

The peer review summary statement for the U01AI151797 application noted that the study was focused on the identification of new, emerging viruses in Southeast Asia, which is a hotspot of viral activity with significant threat to human health. The approach was based on the identification of viral spillovers by means of studying the pathogen in wild animals and performing surveillance targeting high-risk communities.

The peer review summary statement for the U01AI153420 application noted that the study focused on the Nipah virus and aimed to understand why these virus outbreaks appear to only occur in the western part of Bangladesh despite the virus, its bat reservoir, and the primary route of transmission being present throughout the country. It explored human factors, virus temporal dynamics, and pathogenicity and transmissibility of diverse Nipah virus isolates.

APPENDIX D: PRE-AWARD AND AWARD PROCEDURES

NIH addresses potential risks posed by applicants during the pre-award and award process using a risk-based approach that considers factors such as an applicant's financial stability, quality of management systems, history of performance, whether an entity is foreign or domestic, reports and findings from audits, and ability to effectively implement statutory, regulatory, or other requirements imposed on non-Federal entities. Some of the key steps are outlined below.

- NIH uses the electronic Research Administration (eRA),[41] an automated system that maintains all of the checklists, worksheets, and progress reports generated to document the application and review process. In addition, for new or competing continuation grant awards made to a foreign organization or those with a foreign component,[42] NIH obtains the necessary clearances from the Department of State.[43]

- As part of the pre-award process, NIH uses two checklists maintained in eRA to assess grant applicant risk: the Grants Management checklist and the Program checklist. The Grants Management checklist covers topics that address administrative requirements to ensure completeness of an application, compliance with NIH and HHS policies, and compliance with other Federal regulations and requirements. The Program checklist is used to verify compliance with programmatic requirements before the issuance of a competing award and to evaluate the scientific merit of the research.

  When completing the Grants Management checklist, NIH reviews information about an applicant's eligibility, financial integrity, and past performance.[44] Some sources NIH uses include:

  o *GSA SAM.* GSA SAM is an electronic, web-based system that is used to identify parties that are excluded from receiving Federal contracts, certain subcontracts, and other types of Federal financial and nonfinancial assistance and benefits.

  o *The Federal Awardee Performance and Integrity Information System (FAPIIS).* FAPIIS provides publicly available information about an institution's integrity, business ethics, and past performance after receiving a financial assistance award.

---

[41] The eRA is an online interface through which grant applicants, recipients, and Federal staff at NIH can access and share administration information related to research grants.

[42] A foreign component is defined as performance of any significant element or segment of the project outside the United States either by the recipient or by a researcher employed by a foreign organization, whether or not grant funds are expended (NIH GPS, section 16.2).

[43] NIH's Grants Narrative Process Cycle Memorandum, September 30, 2018.

[44] These risk factors are described at 45 CFR § 75.205.

- Once the preparation of an award is complete, eRA generates an Award Worksheet which summarizes the budget and results from the Grants Management and Program checklists. The checklists provide results of an applicant's risk to determine whether issuing awards to an organization is appropriate.

APPENDIX E: NIH GRANT AWARDS TO ECOHEALTH AND ECOHEALTH'S SUBAWARDS

Table 5: Funding Awarded to and Spent by EcoHealth[*]

Award Number	Award Title	Award Amount	Amount Spent
R01AI110964	Understanding the Risk of Bat Coronavirus Emergence	$3,748,715	$3,376,503
U01AI153420	Study of Nipah virus dynamics and genetics in its bat reservoir and of human exposure to NiV across Bangladesh to understand patterns of human outbreaks	1,155,842	478,971
U01AI151797	Understanding Risk of Zoonotic Virus Emergence in EID Hotspots of Southeast Asia	3,052,312	1,529,259
Award and Expenditure Totals		**$7,956,869**	**$5,384,733**

* Grants awarded cover the audit period of FY 2014 to FY 2021. Grant expenditures are as of July 2021, the latest available records at the time the audit fieldwork began.

Table 6: List of NIH Awards to EcoHealth

Issue Date FY	Award Number	Award Title	Budget Year	Action Date	Action Amount
2014	R01AI110964	Understanding the Risk of Bat Coronavirus Emergence	1	5/27/2014	$666,442
2015	R01AI110964	Understanding the Risk of Bat Coronavirus Emergence	2	6/10/2015	630,445
2016	R01AI110964	Understanding the Risk of Bat Coronavirus Emergence	3	7/22/2016	611,090
2017	R01AI110964	Understanding the Risk of Bat Coronavirus Emergence	4	5/26/2017	597,112
2018	R01AI110964	Understanding the Risk of Bat Coronavirus Emergence	5	6/18/2018	581,646
2019	R01AI110964	Understanding the Risk of Bat Coronavirus Emergence	6	7/24/2019	733,750
2019	R01AI110964	Understanding the Risk of Bat Coronavirus Emergence	6	8/5/2019	(71,770)
2020	R01AI110964	Understanding the Risk of Bat Coronavirus Emergence	6	4/27/2020	(369,819)
2020	R01AI110964	Understanding the Risk of Bat Coronavirus Emergence	6	7/13/2020	369,819
				Subtotal	**$3,748,715**
2020	U01AI153420	Study of Nipah virus dynamics and genetics in its bat reservoir and of human exposure to NiV across Bangladesh to understand patterns of human outbreaks	1	9/15/2020	$580,858
2021	U01AI153420	Study of Nipah virus dynamics and genetics in its bat reservoir and of human exposure to NiV across Bangladesh to understand patterns of human outbreaks	2	7/1/2021	574,984
				Subtotal	**$1,155,842**
2020	U01AI151797	Understanding Risk of Zoonotic Virus Emergence in EID Hotspots of Southeast Asia	1	6/17/2020	$1,546,744
2020	U01AI151797	Understanding Risk of Zoonotic Virus Emergence in EID Hotspots of Southeast Asia	1	8/28/2020	0
2021	U01AI151797	Understanding Risk of Zoonotic Virus Emergence in EID Hotspots of Southeast Asia	2	6/11/2021	1,505,568
				Subtotal	**$3,052,312**
			Total Direct NIH Funding to EcoHealth		**$7,956,869**

Table 7: List of EcoHealth's NIH-Funded Subawards*

Subrecipient	Foreign/ Domestic	Funding Agency	Federal Award Number	Federal Award Project Period	Subaward Amount
Wuhan Institute of Virology	Foreign (China)	NIH/NIAID	R01AI110964	06/01/2014 - 05/31/2019	$598,611
Wuhan University School of Public Health	Foreign (China)	NIH/NIAID	R01AI110964	06/01/2014 - 05/31/2019	201,221
Institute of Epidemiology Disease Control and Research	Foreign (Bangladesh)	NIH/NIAID	U01AI153420	09/15/2020 - 06/30/2025	174,186
International Centre for Diarrhoeal Disease Research, Bangladesh	Foreign (Bangladesh)	NIH/NIAID	U01AI153420	09/15/2020 - 06/30/2025	61,853
Henry M. Jackson Foundation	Domestic (Bethesda, MD)	NIH/NIAID	U01AI151797	06/17/2020 - 05/31/2025	114,372
Conservation Medicine	Foreign (Malaysia)	NIH/NIAID	U01AI151797	06/17/2020 - 05/31/2025	241,807
WHO-CC for Research and Training on Viral Zoonoses, Chulalongkorn University	Foreign (Thailand)	NIH/NIAID	U01AI151797	06/17/2020 - 05/31/2025	215,945
The University of North Carolina at Chapel Hill	Domestic (Chapel Hill, NC)	NIH/NIAID	U01AI151797	06/17/2020 - 05/31/2025	194,375
Total of EcoHealth's NIH-Funded Subawards					**$1,802,370**

* These subawards were in place during the audit period from FY 2014 through FY 2021 and represented the subawards for which EcoHealth had expenditures as of July 2021, the latest available accounting records from EcoHealth at the time the audit fieldwork began.

APPENDIX F: FEDERAL REQUIREMENTS FOR TERMINATING AND SUSPENDING GRANT AWARDS

According to HHS regulations (45 CFR § 75.372), a grant award may be terminated by the:

- HHS awarding agency if the non-Federal entity fails to comply with the terms and conditions of the award;

- HHS awarding agency for cause;

- HHS awarding agency with the consent of the non-Federal entity, in which case the two parties must agree upon the termination conditions including the effective date and, in the case of partial termination, the portion to be terminated; or

- non-Federal entity upon sending to the HHS awarding agency written notification setting forth the reasons for such termination, the effective date, and, in the case of partial termination, the portion to be terminated.

Furthermore, HHS regulations (45 CFR § 75.374) require HHS awarding agencies to provide a non-Federal entity an opportunity to object and provide information and documentation challenging the suspension or termination actions according to written process and procedures published by the HHS awarding agency. The HHS awarding agency must comply with any requirements for hearings, appeals, or other administrative proceedings to which the non-Federal entity is entitled under any statute or regulation.

NIH GPS Section 8.7 covers grant appeals procedures. It requires the formal notification of an adverse determination to contain a statement of the recipient's appeal rights and indicates that there be an NIH official specified in the notification. Furthermore, if the first level NIH review of an appeal is adverse to the recipient, or if a recipient's request for review is rejected, the recipient has an option to submit a request to the HHS Departmental Appeals Board for further review within 30 days after receiving the final NIH decision.

APPENDIX G: FEDERAL REQUIREMENTS FOR SUBRECIPIENT MONITORING

According to 45 CFR § 75.342, non-Federal entities are responsible for oversight of the operations of Federal award-supported activities. The non-Federal entity must monitor its activities under Federal awards to assure compliance with applicable Federal requirements and performance expectations are being achieved. Monitoring by the non-Federal entity must cover each program, function, or activity. Events may occur between the scheduled performance reporting dates that have significant impact upon the supported activity. In such cases, the non-Federal entity must inform the HHS awarding agency or pass-through entity as soon as the following types of conditions become known: problems, delays, or adverse conditions that will materially impair the ability to meet the objective of the Federal award. This disclosure must include a statement of the action taken, or contemplated, and any assistance needed to resolve the situation.

Pursuant to 45 CFR § 75.352(d), EcoHealth in its role as a pass-through entity must monitor the activities of a subrecipient as necessary to ensure: (1) the subaward is used for authorized purposes in compliance with Federal statutes, regulations, and the terms and conditions of the subaward; and (2) subaward performance goals are achieved. Pass-through entity monitoring of the subrecipient must include:

- reviewing financial and performance reports required by the pass-through entity;

- following up and ensuring that the subrecipient takes timely and appropriate action on all deficiencies pertaining to the Federal award provided to the subrecipient from the pass-through entity detected through audits, on-site reviews, and other means;

- issuing a management decision for audit findings pertaining to the Federal award provided to the subrecipient from the pass-through entity as required by 45 CFR § 75.521;

- depending upon the pass-through entity's assessment of risk posed by the subrecipient (as described in paragraph (b) of this section), using monitoring tools that may be useful for the pass-through entity to ensure proper accountability and compliance with program requirements and achievement of performance goals, including:

  o providing the subrecipient with training and technical assistance on program-related matters and

  o performing onsite reviews of the subrecipient's program operations; and

- considering whether the results of the subrecipient's audits, on-site reviews, or other monitoring indicate conditions that necessitate adjustments to the pass-through entity's own records; and

- considering taking enforcement action against noncompliant subrecipients as described in 45 CFR § 75.371 and in program regulations.

APPENDIX H: SUBRECIPIENT AGREEMENTS LACKED REQUIRED DATA ELEMENTS

Table 8: Required Data Element and Number of Instances of Noncompliance From Reviewing 11 Subrecipient Agreements Pursuant to 45 CFR § 75.352(a)(1)

Required Data Element	Number of Instances of Noncompliance
Subrecipient's Name	No Instances
Subrecipient's Unique Entity Identifier	No Instances
Federal Award Identification Number	11 Instances
Federal Award Date of Award to the Recipient by the HHS Awarding Agency	11 Instances
Subaward Period of Performance Start and End Dates	No Instances
Amount of Federal Funds Obligated by This Action by the Pass-Through Entity to the Subrecipient	No Instances
Total Amount of Federal Funds Obligated to the Subrecipient by the Pass-Through Entity Including the Current Obligation	11 Instances
Total Amount of the Federal Award Committed to the Subrecipient by the Pass-Through Entity	11 Instances
Federal Award Project Description as Required by FFATA	No Instances
Name of HHS Awarding Agency, Pass-Through Entity, and Contact Information for Awarding Official of the Pass-Through Entity	10 Instances
Code of Federal Domestic Assistance (CFDA) Number and Name; the Pass-Through Entity Must Identify the Dollar Amount Made Available Under Each Federal Award and the CFDA Number at the Time of Disbursement	10 Instances
Identification of Whether the Award Is Research and Development	11 Instances
Indirect Cost Rate for the Federal Award	4 Instances

APPENDIX I: NATIONAL INSTITUTES OF HEALTH COMMENTS

DEPARTMENT OF HEALTH & HUMAN SERVICES   Public Health Service

National Institutes of Health
Bethesda, Maryland 20892
www.nih.gov

DATE: December 20, 2022

TO: Juliet T. Hodgkins
Principal Deputy Inspector General

FROM: Acting Principal Deputy Director, National Institutes of Health

SUBJECT: NIH Comments on Draft Report, *"The National Institutes of Health and EcoHealth Alliance Did Not Effectively Monitor Awards and Subawards, Resulting in Missed Opportunities to Oversee Research and Other Deficiencies"* (A-05-21-00025)

Attached are the National Institutes of Health's (NIH) comments on the draft Office of Inspector General's (OIG) report, *"The National Institutes of Health and EcoHealth Alliance Did Not Effectively Monitor Awards and Subawards, Resulting in Missed Opportunities to Oversee Research and Other Deficiencies"* (A-05-21-00025).

NIH appreciates the review conducted by OIG and the opportunity to provide the clarifications on this draft report. If you have questions or concerns, please contact Meredith Stein in the Office of Management Assessment at 301-402-8482.

/s/

Tara A. Schwetz, Ph.D.

Attachments

GENERAL COMMENTS OF THE NATIONAL INSTITUTES OF HEALTH (NIH) ON THE DEPARTMENT OF HEALTH AND HUMAN SERVICES (HHS) OFFICE OF INSPECTOR GENERAL (OIG) DRAFT REPORT ENTITLED: "THE NATIONAL INSTITUTES OF HEALTH AND ECOHEALTH ALLIANCE DID NOT EFFECTIVELY MONITOR AWARDS AND SUBAWARDS, RESULTING IN MISSED OPPORTUNITIES TO OVERSEE RESEARCH AND OTHER DEFICIENCIES" (A-05-21-00025)

The National Institutes of Health (NIH) appreciates the review conducted by the Office of Inspector General (OIG) and the opportunity to provide clarifications on this draft report. NIH respectfully submits the following general comments.

OIG Recommendation 1:
We recommend that the National Institutes of Health ensure that EcoHealth accurately and in a timely manner reports award and subaward information, including in:
- Recipient progress reports;
- The Federal Funding Accountability and Transparency Act of 2006, Subawarding Reporting System; and
- Recipient-audited financial statements

NIH Response:
NIH concurs with OIG's finding and corresponding recommendation that NIH ensure that EcoHealth accurately and in a timely manner reports award and subaward information.

- In its August 19, 2022, letter to EcoHealth, NIH stipulated for R01AI110964 the following Specific Award Conditions, similar to Specific Award Conditions already implemented for other NIH grants awarded to EcoHealth.
  - EcoHealth must conduct or arrange for the conduct of onsite subrecipient facility inspections every 6 months to ensure that subaward activities are being properly executed.
  - EcoHealth must provide NIH with copies of updated subaward agreements for R01AI110964 that correct the deficiencies noted in the table above and demonstrate compliance with the NIH GPS 15.2.1 Written Agreement. The subaward agreements must state the correct F&A rate which, for foreign subrecipients is 8% (see NIH GPS 16.6).
  - The expanded authority for automatic no-cost extensions will be withdrawn. This will require that EcoHealth request and receive written prior approval from the National Institute of Allergy and Infectious Diseases (NIAID) before any extensions of the final budget period.
  - Automatic carryover authorities will be withdrawn. This will require EcoHealth to request and receive written approval to carry over any unobligated balances on all awards prior to carrying over unobligated balances from one budget period to any subsequent budget period.
  - EcoHealth is required to submit semi-annual RPPRs and Federal Financial Reports to NIAID.
  - EcoHealth will provide NIAID with copies of FSRS reporting for all subawards issued under the revised R01AI119064.

1

- These specific award conditions will be in place for a period of at least 3 years from the date of the revised Notice of Award with an annual review to ensure proper compliance.

OIG Recommendation 2:
We recommend that the National Institutes of Health implement enhanced monitoring, documentation, and reporting requirements for recipients with foreign subrecipients.

NIH Response:
NIH generally concurs with OIG's finding and the corresponding recommendation.

NIH will evaluate how best to consider the OIG recommendation within the framework of 2 C.F.R. §§ 200.331 - 200.333, Subrecipient Monitoring and Management (Uniform Administrative Regulations). NIH will also need to consider 2 CFR 200.100(c), which states that "The Federal awarding agency may adjust requirements to a class of Federal awards or non-Federal entities when approved by the Office of Management and Budget...."

NIH will also evaluate best practices across government for overseeing awards issued to domestic recipients who in turn oversee foreign subrecipients. The results of this evaluation are anticipated to inform how NIH may implement the OIG recommendation.

OIG Recommendation 3:
We recommend that the National Institutes of Health define the process and timeline for what NIH considers "immediate notification" as it relates to specific award conditions intended to report unexpected research outcomes.

NIH Response:
NIH concurs with OIG's finding and corresponding recommendation.

Within 90 days of the publication of this report, NIH will issue a Guide Notice and revise the NIH Grants Policy Statement to include a definition for the process and timeline for "immediate notification" as it relates to specific award conditions intended to report unexpected research outcomes.

OIG Recommendation 4:
We recommend that the National Institutes of Health ensure that administrative actions such as terminations are performed in compliance with Federal regulations and HHS policies and procedures, and appropriate notifications of appeal rights are provided.

2

GENERAL COMMENTS OF THE NATIONAL INSTITUTES OF HEALTH (NIH) ON THE DEPARTMENT OF HEALTH AND HUMAN SERVICES (HHS) OFFICE OF INSPECTOR GENERAL (OIG) DRAFT REPORT ENTITLED: "THE NATIONAL INSTITUTES OF HEALTH AND ECOHEALTH ALLIANCE DID NOT EFFECTIVELY MONITOR AWARDS AND SUBAWARDS, RESULTING IN MISSED OPPORTUNITIES TO OVERSEE RESEARCH AND OTHER DEFICIENCIES" (A-05-21-00025)

NIH Response:
NIH concurs with OIG's finding and corresponding recommendation.

NIH will ensure that administrative actions such as terminations are performed in compliance with Federal regulations and the Department of Health and Human Services (HHS) policies and procedures, and appropriate notifications of appeal rights are provided.

OIG Recommendation 5:
We recommend that the National Institutes of Health work with EcoHealth to recover identified unallowable costs, along with salary costs in excess of the NIH salary cap and bonus costs that were not sampled.

NIH Response:
NIH concurs with OIG's finding and corresponding recommendation.

Within 90 days of the publication of this report, NIH will work with EcoHealth to recover identified unallowable costs, along with salary costs in excess of the NIH salary cap and bonus costs that were not sampled.

OIG Recommendation 6:
We recommend that the National Institutes of Health work with EcoHealth to determine whether EcoHealth had any unreimbursed costs at the time award R01AI110964 was terminated.

NIH Response:
NIH concurs with OIG's finding and corresponding recommendation.

Within 90 days of the publication of this report, NIH will work with EcoHealth to determine whether EcoHealth had any unreimbursed costs at the time award R01AI110964 was terminated.

OIG Recommendation 7:
We recommend that the National Institutes of Health assess whether NIAID staff are following the NIAID P3CO policy, including erring on the side of inclusion when determining whether proposed research should be referred to the NIAID DURC/P3CO Committee for research proposals that may involve PPP.

NIH Response:
NIH concurs with OIG's finding and corresponding recommendation.

The National Science Advisory Board for Biosecurity (NSABB) is currently charged with evaluating and providing recommendations to the Office of Science and Technology Policy (OSTP) and HHS on the effectiveness of the current oversight framework for research involving

3

GENERAL COMMENTS OF THE NATIONAL INSTITUTES OF HEALTH (NIH) ON THE DEPARTMENT OF HEALTH AND HUMAN SERVICES (HHS) OFFICE OF INSPECTOR GENERAL (OIG) DRAFT REPORT ENTITLED: "THE NATIONAL INSTITUTES OF HEALTH AND ECOHEALTH ALLIANCE DID NOT EFFECTIVELY MONITOR AWARDS AND SUBAWARDS, RESULTING IN MISSED OPPORTUNITIES TO OVERSEE RESEARCH AND OTHER DEFICIENCIES" (A-05-21-00025)

enhanced potential pandemic pathogens (ePPPs). The NIH has established a Working Group of the NSABB to address this charge. As part of its evaluation, the NSABB will assess the current process adopted by HHS (including NIH and NIAID) for the review and oversight of proposed research involving ePPPs.

OIG Recommendation 8:
We recommend that the National Institutes of Health based on information provided in this audit and other information available to NIH, consider whether it is appropriate to refer WIV to HHS for debarment and exercise continued monitoring and enforcement activities as appropriate over the course of the grant awards and subawards.

NIH Response:
NIH concurs with OIG's finding and corresponding recommendation.

NIH notes that debarment decisions are made by the HHS Suspension and Debarment Official, not NIH, and that any proposed debarments are subject to the Office of Management and Budget (OMB) guidelines to agencies on governmentwide debarment and suspension (nonprocurement) in 2 CFR 180.

OIG Recommendation 9:
We recommend that the National Institutes of Health ensure for any future NIH grant awards that EcoHealth has addressed the deficiencies noted in the report.

NIH Response:
NIH concurs with OIG's finding and corresponding recommendation.

In its August 19, 2022, letter to EcoHealth, NIH stated, "the NIH reserves the right to take additional compliance actions as needed, such as disallowing funds or imposing additional specific award conditions, if the HHS Office of Inspector General identifies other noncompliance and/or recommends such actions as a result of its audit of EcoHealth." Therefore, within 90 days of the publication of this report, NIH will work with EcoHealth to ensure that the deficiencies noted in this report are being satisfactorily addressed.

4

APPENDIX J: ECOHEALTH COMMENTS

EcoHealth Alliance

22 December 2022

Sheri L. Fulcher
Regional Inspector General for Audit Services
Office of Audit Services, Region V
233 North Michigan, Suite 1360
Chicago, IL 60601

Re: Report Number. (A-05-21-00025)

Dear Ms. Fulcher,

Thank you for providing a draft of the report entitled *The National Institutes of Health and EcoHealth Alliance Did Not Effectively Monitor Awards and Subawards, Resulting in Missed Opportunities to Oversee Research and Other Deficiencies.* This letter represents an overview of our responses to the Findings and Recommendations. (Detailed comments, keyed to specific issues, are contained in the attached Appendix.)

This OIG audit report covers National Institute of Health (NIH) and EcoHealth Alliance (EHA) compliance with Federal requirements to ensure proper monitoring and use of grant funds for three NIH awards to EHA totaling approximately $8.0 million for the period covering FY2014 through FY2021. The OIG audit objectives were to determine whether: (1) NIH monitored grants to EHA in accordance with Federal requirements; and (2) whether EHA used and managed its NIH grant funds in accordance with Federal requirements. **EHA welcomes the OIG oversight and has collaborated fully and transparently with this audit.**

We note that the OIG did not find significant issues with EHA's grant oversight and compliance, summarizing its findings as follows: "EcoHealth had steps in place to conduct risk assessments of its subrecipients, and also had standardized checklists to document routine monitoring of its subrecipients." EHA accepts OIG's recommendations on how to ensure that subawards are compliant with Federal requirements; how to ensure compliance with subrecipient monitoring and reporting; and how to comply better with certain public disclosure requirements associated with reporting subaward funding. In fact, **EHA had already corrected certain procedures addressed by the OIG during the time period covered by the audit, or corrected them once we were notified of a finding by the OIG audit team.**

We note the additional DHHS OIG audit team finding that EHA "did not always use its grant funds in accordance with Federal requirements, resulting in $89,171 in unallowable costs." This amounts to roughly 1% of the NIH grants awarded to EHA: put another way, **the OIG found that EHA did comply with Federal requirements 99% of the time**.

EHA has already reimbursed the NIH for the total in unallowable costs as determined by the OIG. We found the OIG analysis instructive in several cases where EHA did not follow the appropriate requirement (in two cases these involved expenses as small as a $19 overpayment and a miscoded $5 beverage) and have corrected these minor errors. In other cases, EHA disagrees with the OIG interpretation of the Federal requirements and we are seeking clarification on these instances with the NIH.

During the audit process, we discovered that EHA has been underpaid by the NIH for indirect cost allocation equivalent to $126,391. The OIG notes this in the report and EHA has pursued reimbursement of these funds owed to EHA by the NIH.

There were only two substantive areas of disagreement with the OIG over their findings – one concerning the timeliness of EHA's progress Year 5 Progress report on a R01 grant from NIAID, the other an issue around whether an experiment that showed unexpected levels of genome copies at an early stage constituted "enhanced growth" that required further review. We do not agree with the OIG's characterization of these two issues, for reasons outlined in detail in the Appendix.

During the 8-year period covered by this OIG audit, the Federal requirements changed multiple times, and EHA policies changed to match them. Many of the findings occurred under a different management team. Additionally, the OIG audit does not reflect a series of new requirements placed on EHA contracts by NIH that have already been put in place and set standards that are above and beyond the normal procedures for subrecipients.

The audit process has helped EHA to sharpen its policies and practices to enable even better compliance with NIH and other Federal rules in the future. We appreciate the professionalism of the OIG review staff and the analysis provided in your report.

Sincerely,

Peter Daszak, PhD
President, EcoHealth Alliance
520 Eighth Avenue, Suite 1200
New York, NY 10018, USA
www.ecohealthalliance.org

APPENDIX:
EcoHealth Alliance responses to DHHS OIG audit report recommendations[*]

A. *We recommend that EcoHealth Alliance:*

1.   *prepare subaward and consultant agreements that contain all required information and are accurate,*

EcoHealth Alliance Response: We agree with this recommendation and have already instituted measures to correct omissions on contracts and agreements. Many of the instances identified by DHHS OIG were from over 5 years ago and were copy-paste errors resulting from inadvertent reuse of a prior contract template. EcoHealth Alliance has updated and revised all its subaward and consultant agreements to contain required language and subaward identification.

2.   *submit progress reports by the required due date,*

EcoHealth Alliance Response: EcoHealth Alliance will continue to submit all required annual, semi-annual, or other progress reports by the deadlines set by NIH, to the best of our ability. The DHHS OIG report suggests that EcoHealth Alliance submitted its R01-AI110964 Year 5 progress report late, and that the report indicates 'enhanced growth' of a recombinant virus in an approved experiment. We refute this statement: it does not provide a full review of the facts. We have provided extensive documentation to NIH and to the DHHS OIG to support this point (see below).

Regarding the timely submission of our report: **EcoHealth Alliance's Year 5 progress report was written and uploaded into the NIH online portal for submission by EcoHealth Alliance staff in July 2019 -- ahead of the September deadline.** When EcoHealth Alliance staff attempted officially to submit the report during late July 2019, the grant had been renewed (24 July 2019) for an additional 5 years and the NIH system locked EcoHealth Alliance out from submitting a Year 5 report. NIH staff did not follow up with a request to EcoHealth Alliance for a Year 5 report, despite frequent communication among EcoHealth Alliance staff and NIH program and grants management staff during that time. Direct questions from EcoHealth Alliance staff remained unanswered by NIH, and phone calls were not returned. The fact that the new award was made, work was allowed to continue, and no requests for an official Year 5 report submission were made by NIH, suggested to EcoHealth Alliance staff that we were in compliance. The next communication on this issue from NIH was on 23 July 2021, approximately two years later, requesting submission of the Year 5 report. EcoHealth rapidly complied and submitted its Year 5 report within 11 days, but only after considerable intervention from NIH staff to circumvent its system's lockout. Even though the grant was terminated and

---

[*] Text in italics in this Appendix is quoted verbatim from the DHHS OIG Draft Report Findings and Recommendations.

then suspended, and no funding was available to work on the progress reports, EcoHealth Alliance continued to comply with NIH reporting requests and has submitted a Year 6 and Year 7 report on this grant.

Regarding the allegation that the report indicated 'enhanced growth' of a recombinant virus:

3. *comply with requirements to immediately notify NIH of conditions that materially impact the ability to meet award objectives,*

EcoHealth Alliance Response: To the best of its ability, EcoHealth Alliance will continue to comply with requirements to notify NIH of conditions that materially impact its ability to meet award objectives, and to do this in a timely manner, and as directed. However, we refute the suggestion that EcoHealth Alliance failed to comply with the timeliness of reporting or of conditions that materially affect the award objectives.

Firstly, on the issue of the timing of our reporting the results of coronavirus experiments to NIH: As we have already indicated to the DHHS OIG with documentary evidence in support, and in previous letters to NIH, NIH did not use the phrase 'immediately notify' in the document of record for the amended annual award – the Notice of Award. Additionally, NIH failed to provide a timeframe for notification in either the letter indicating that these experiments were approved, or in the NIH Notice of Award. Finally, we did, in fact, notify NIH in a timely manner about these results, having provided this information rapidly after being sent it by the laboratory that conducted the experiments in China.

Secondly, on the issue of the material nature of the experimental findings in the report: DHHS OIG states that "*according to NIH's evaluation of EcoHealth's progress report for Year 5 of the grant, NIH believed there was evidence that the research conducted by EcoHealth's subrecipient WIV during Year 5 resulted in enhanced growth by more than one log, thus triggering the special term and condition to immediately notify NIAID and potentially requiring the research to undergo review under the HHS P3CO Framework.*" **This statement is not factually correct and EcoHealth Alliance has provided both a detailed explanation and documentation to both the NIH and the DHHS OIG to support EcoHealth Alliance's statement. The contention that EcoHealth Alliance failed to report "enhanced growth" that would have required additional P3CO review as "gain of function" research is based on a misinterpretation of what the experiment in question actually showed.**

Specifically, EcoHealth Alliance reported on the same experiment in its Year 4 report submitted on time in 2018 and at that time (25 April 2018) EcoHealth Alliance emailed a copy of its submitted Year 4 report to NIH and requested a timeslot to discuss the Year 4 report, the planned Year 5 work, and a renewal proposal. This call happened on 18 July 2018. **At no time then or until well after this grant was terminated in April 2020, was there any comment from NIH re. experimental results or the timing of reporting.** Additionally, as indicated in our letter to NIH October 26th 2021, and in our extensive responses to the DHHS OIG's earlier drafts of this report, in virological terms, "virus growth" normally refers to viral titer measuring the concentration of infectious viruses by plaque assay. The experiment we reported to NIH actually shows genome copies per gram, not viral titers. We have been advised by senior virologists that data on genome copies per gram usually do not accurately equate to viral titer, since genomic material from inactivated, incompletely formed, or dead virus are also measured. Viral titers were not measured in the experiments detailed in the Year 4 or 5 reports. We also note that the genome copy data for recombinant viruses are only enhanced relative to the WIV1 backbone at the earliest part of the experiment and by the endpoint, there was no discernably significant difference among the different viral types, suggesting that these differences, if real, were transient. Given the small number of mice used, it is also uncertain whether the survival and weight loss data were statistically relevant, and as no further replications of this experiment were performed, we are unable to corroborate these initial results. We assume that these were the rationale NIH used at the time for not highlighting this work as requiring further clarification or secondary review under the "gain of function" guidelines.

4. *ensure that it has the ability to access all records related to its research conducted at subrecipient locations,*

EcoHealth Alliance Response: To the best of its ability, EcoHealth Alliance will continue to do all possible to ensure that it can access and supply all records related to its research conducted at subrecipient locations. However, EcoHealth Alliance finds the DHHS OIG report statement misleading in suggesting that EcoHealth Alliance was simply *"unable to obtain scientific documentation from a subrecipient"*. It is correct that on 5 November 2021 NIH wrote to EcoHealth Alliance requesting scientific documentation from its subrecipient, the Wuhan Institute of Virology (WIV). These included lab notebooks and the original data used to produce graphs for the year 4 and 5 reports to NIH. However, DHHS OIG omitted the following critical information: 1) 18 months prior to this request (on 19 April 2020) NIH instructed EcoHealth Alliance "to cease providing any funds from the above noted grant to the WIV", and that EcoHealth Alliance responded on 21st April 2020 to confirm that no funds had been sent to WIV under the award, nor had any contract been signed, and that EcoHealth Alliance would comply with all NIH's requirements; 2) NIH terminated the award on 24th April 2020 "for convenience"; 3) during 2020 and 2021, the WIV, EcoHealth Alliance, and the research that NIH funded became subject to significant geopolitical pressure and almost daily misreporting in the media globally, including repeated unsubstantiated allegations that lab notebooks had been hidden, or forged, or data corrupted, and these acts covered up. During that time, EcoHealth Alliance was subjected to political attacks in the USA and abroad, including efforts to remove our eligibility for federal funding based on disinformation and hearsay.

NIH's request for documentation 18 months after a project was de-funded, terminated and then suspended, and the intense media and political pressure are extraordinary circumstances that should be noted in the report. These conditions and particularly the political tensions between the Chinese and US governments at the time effectively shut down communications among scientists at the WIV (a Chinese government laboratory) and EcoHealth Alliance staff, making it impossible for EcoHealth Alliance to secure the requested data. Despite this, and as DHHS OIG notes, EcoHealth Alliance made reasonable attempts to comply with NIH's requests, including supplying further unpublished data. EcoHealth Alliance also forwarded the request to WIV staff, but has not yet received a response.

EcoHealth Alliance always has and continues routinely to share its unpublished data from its research with its NIH program officers through regular progress reports. Genetic sequences relevant to EcoHealth Alliance's work are routinely deposited in the NIH GenBank so that they can be used by other scientists globally. Indeed, even after NIH terminated EcoHealth Alliance's award, EcoHealth Alliance continued to file annual reports with NIH to provide unpublished data. In addition, EcoHealth Alliance submitted analyses of the NIH-supported work for publication in leading international peer-reviewed journals so that the data and results are available publicly.

5. *properly identify subawards in financial statements, and*

EcoHealth Alliance Response: Prior to 2019, our CPA consultant advised EcoHealth Alliance not to list foreign subawards in financial statements. We have provided documentation to DHHS OIG to confirm that this was the professional advice we received. Notwithstanding this advice, for the past 3-years, EcoHealth Alliance has provided full subaward identification in all internal and public financial statements and has instituted policies to ensure this will continue to be our practice.

6. *disclose subawards according to FFATA requirements.*

EcoHealth Alliance Response: EcoHealth Alliance has provided all required FFATA reporting forms since NIH first requested these documents. Copies of FFATA reporting for all subawards have been provided to NIH upon request and at NIH's current direction continue to be provided to NIH 30 days following EcoHealth Alliance's submissions to the FFATA system.

B. We recommend EcoHealth Alliance refund to the Government $89,171 in unallowable costs consisting of:

EcoHealth Alliance Response: EcoHealth Alliance has already refunded this amount to NIH in full. However, we note that during our review of financial records as part of this audit, we identified $126,391 in allowable costs on three NIH awards that have not yet been reimbursed to EcoHealth Alliance. At NIH's request, on 16 December 2022, EcoHealth Alliance provided details of these unreimbursed costs, which we expect to recover in due course.

Despite our repayment of the $89,171 in costs that DHHS OIG has claimed are unallowable, EcoHealth Alliance maintains our previously-stated opinion that some of these expenditures are 'allowable' and others are reasonably disputed. We have provided rationale for this in the detailed responses below:

1. *salary costs claimed in excess of the NIH salary cap totaling $10,627,*

EcoHealth Alliance Response: EcoHealth Alliance has reimbursed this amount to NIH and agrees with DHHS OIG's finding here. EcoHealth Alliance made minor miscalculations in the time allotment of allowable salaries over the NIH GPS 4.2.10 Salary Cap/Salary Limitation. To address this EcoHealth Alliance employed a new time management system and software that accurately captures and segregates all salary charges for NIH funded personnel that exceed Salary Cap/Salary Limitations.

2. *bonus costs totaling $15,977,*

EcoHealth Alliance Response: EcoHealth Alliance has reimbursed this amount to NIH. Nonetheless, EcoHealth Alliance disagrees with the DHHS OIG interpretation of *NIH GPS 7.9.1 Allowability of Costs/Activities*, which clearly allows bonus and incentive payments to be reimbursed by NIH. EcoHealth Alliance maintains that its policy of providing such payments to staff is: 1) based on performance and therefore referred to as providing "incentive payments"; 2) based on an "established plan" clearly indicated in the EcoHealth Alliance Employee Handbook; 3) established as an EcoHealth Alliance Board-approved operating procedure for more than 12 years; and 4) something that staff are made fully aware of *prior to* their performance (i.e. 'services rendered'). EcoHealth Alliance has received legal counsel corroborating its understanding that EcoHealth Alliance staff incentive payment allocations may be deemed "allowable" under existing Federal guidelines, and are in accord with standard criteria for interpreting and applying a statute or regulation.

3. *indirect and fringe benefits associated with salary and bonus costs totaling $17,836,*

EcoHealth Alliance Response: EcoHealth Alliance has reimbursed NIH for this expense. Nonetheless, EcoHealth Alliance disputes the portion of indirect and fringe corresponding to DHHS OIG's determination about the allowability of incentive payments to EcoHealth Alliance staff.

4. *Ph.D. education tuition costs totaling $13,951 and associated indirect costs of $4,641,*

EcoHealth Alliance Response: EcoHealth Alliance has reimbursed NIH for this expense. Nonetheless, EcoHealth Alliance disagrees with the DHHS OIG understanding of NIH GPS 7.9.1 Allowability of Costs/Activities that tuition payments are an unallowable cost. This staff member and graduate student is undergoing training in research methodology as part of a doctoral program that is precisely the scope and type of research and work conducted on the respective NIH funded project. EcoHealth Alliance believes this is an allowable cost because: 1) the staff member is conducting activities necessary to the Federal award; 2) the expense was incurred in accordance with established EcoHealth Alliance policies; 3) the tuition payments are reasonable and fair; 4) the employee is not 'attending Kingston University', since the graduate program is a part-time 'external candidate' PhD program with no required courses and all by research and thesis.

5. *indirect costs totaling $13,037 claimed by a subrecipient,*

EcoHealth Alliance Response: EcoHealth Alliance has reimbursed NIH for this expense. This was a simple error regarding the *de minimis* overhead rate for a foreign subrecipient on a contract dating back to 2015. US Federal agencies apply different *de minimis* rates and this error was the result of using a single contract template based on an agency that allows a 10% rate on foreign subrecipients, versus the 8% allowed by NIH.

6. *travel costs totaling $5,752 and associated indirect costs of $1,876,*

EcoHealth Alliance Response: EcoHealth Alliance has reimbursed these costs to NIH. Two of these were simple miscoding errors. However, one travel cost in the amount of $2,808.43 is a valid allowable cost. At the time of travel (2016), the printed receipt for this approved, budgeted foreign travel expense was lost. EcoHealth Alliance now has a back-up system for receipt storage or capture and a policy for rapid follow-up with vendors to secure missing receipts, however that was not our policy at the time. When DHHS OIG requested this receipt in 2021, EcoHealth Alliance contacted the non-USA-based vendor, but this over-4-year-old expense was no longer on file with the vendor. We submitted corroborating documentation to DHHS OIG, including verified price estimates, the number of travelers/participants, and meeting-agendas. However, DHHS OIG did not consider these sufficient.

7. *visa costs of $2,500 and associated indirect costs of $896,*

EcoHealth Alliance Response: EcoHealth Alliance has reimbursed NIH for this expense. Nonetheless, EcoHealth Alliance disputes this finding. Expedited H1-B visa processing times take 15 business days. Regular H1-B processing times take between 3-to-6 months. At the time of this expenditure, due to the COVID-19 pandemic, regular processing times were further delayed. EcoHealth Alliance considered expedited visa expense justifiable given the need to rapidly engage an employee with a highly specialized skill set and background to work on a pandemic-delayed project during lock-down at the end of 2020.

8. *subaward costs of $2,052, and*

EcoHealth Alliance Response: EcoHealth Alliance agrees with this finding. This was a miscalculation on the part of EcoHealth Alliance's subaward in 2015 and was an error not noted at the time by the subaward or EcoHealth Alliance personnel. Since that time, we have instituted redundancy and cross checks in subaward receipts and processing and a commercial receipt storage and capture system that will reduce the opportunity for similar mistakes.

9. *professional fees costs of $19 and associated indirect costs of $7.*

EcoHealth Alliance Response: EcoHealth Alliance agrees with this finding. This was a copy-paste error on the part of program personnel. We have since instituted an internal third review of all payment requests submitted to our finance team to reduce the opportunity for similar mistakes.